A Face Of Anxiety

Trish Barillas

Cover / Back Image: Chad Wagner

2

Preface

This book originated from an Instabook, which is a series of posts I put up on my Instagram account @afaceofanxiety, which reads as a normal book would, just in cliff notes style. I'm by no means a doctor or a licensed Psychologist or Psychiatrist.

I'm a certified Life Coach, practicing for over a decade, who happens to suffer from severe anxiety/panic disorder. This book is to show others that it is possible to live a fulfilled and positive life with mental illness. My only hope is to help you on your journey towards embracing and accepting a life with anxiety.

Acknowledgements

I want to thank my Mom, Dad and sister Pie Barillas for always accepting me as is. My friends Karma, Summer and Melissa who have helped in making me become a more holistic and grounded human. Sidney & Maxine Kahn, who made dreams a reality for my family and me.

For my amazing team of healers: Andrew Chiodo LCSW (Therapist), Robert Paul Johnson L.AC (Acupuncturist) and David Dowd (Life coach).

To Jose Antonio Hernandez for giving me the Instabook idea, which has now become an actual book. To all the staff at Lenox Hill Hospitals and Penny McDermott for the best care and service an anxiety sufferer could have asked for.

Lastly to Ms Mia, who has been on this crazy journey with me for the past 15 years. Although she scares the hell out of most people, she has always comforted me in times of distress. Some may call her the devil cat but I call her my service kitty.

Contents

Chapter 1

Where I Am Now

"My dysfunction has

now become my

function"

Luckily for me, I was seated next to a motivational speaker, Victor Antonio, on my flight to New Zealand to visit my sister, whom I call "Peepee." (Her actual name is Piedad, exactly why she got the nicknames Pie and Peepee.) Victor and I were bucket-seat neighbors for the long, thirteen-hour flight to Auckland. We started talking to one another before takeoff, as I was telling him about the functions of our chairs and whatnot. Victor was incredibly easy to talk to, given his career, so the two of us were just chatting up a storm. What Victor didn't know was that he was seated next to someone with severe acute anxiety/panic disorder. I fly quite often, and they say it gets easier, but I call bullshit on that statement. Anxiety is interesting because it comes and goes just like the tides. Some days are great, and some are just a punch in the face. This would be one of those latter days. Flying is a huge trigger for my anxiety, and because I know this, I'm always prepared with some Xanax in my bag. About forty minutes into the flight, I started to feel that wave of anxiety, but this time, just for some extra fun, it was a full-blown panic attack. I went from zero to one hundred real quick and not in a cool-rap-song kind of way.

Victor had to rub my back, grab some throw-up bags, and speak to the airline attendants to inform them that I was suffering from a panic attack. My poor bucket-seat neighbor now became my caretaker. Let's just say, anyone who gives up their throw-up bag for you and gets you ice chips is a friend for life, and the two of you are forever connected. Safe to say, after taking a recommended amount of Xanax, nine hours later, I came back to life. Victor, who had to give a speech that day, didn't sleep one bit, fearing that I would need his assistance again. He also gave me his blanket. Victor is a godsend, and I am so thankful that people like him exist in the world—those who are willing to place their needs aside to help others in distress.

Aside from these minor blips that will always occur, I am living life to the fullest, despite the anxiety disorder. Trust me, it took years to comprehend and adjust to the disorder. I won't pretend like any of it was easy, which is why I'm writing this book, hoping that it will bring some insight or comfort to those who are struggling with this type of disorder, or any disorder for that matter.

But enough about my anxiety for now; let me tell you a little about myself. I currently reside in Chelsea, Manhattan, with my fat cat, Ms. Mia. We've been living in NYC for the past fifteen years. I am blessed with amazing friends and a very vast social life. There is nothing I would change about my life, not even my anxiety. Currently, I'm pursuing my dream job with my passion project in full swing (the book you're reading). Right about now, something needs to be said about timing, experience, and maturity. It took me years to understand my disorder, and then even more years to learn myself. The disorder was the easier of the two to figure out since it has a lot to do with genetics, chemical makeup, anatomy, and what you place in your body. Understanding myself is still a work in progress, but so far, I know who I am, what I stand for, and what my intentions are.

So who am I? Glad you asked. (P.S. I'm a talker, in case you haven't already figured that out by now.) I'm an independent woman, a first-generation Guatemalan, a ride-or-die friend, an animal lover, a charity advocate, a lover of everything Dyson, a ballet dancer, a Ducati rider, a tequila/whiskey/wine drinker, and an anxiety survivor with strong family values and OCD tendencies who is outspoken and tech savvy and loves a good business challenge. These are just a few of the things that make me who I am today, and they are what I am most proud of. Now comes the "How can you be proud to have anxiety?" part. Well easy, because I wouldn't be a lot of those things I mentioned if it wasn't for my disorder. It's interesting to note that when you're finally coming to grips with anxiety and you're about to start treatment; you become concerned that the parts that made you "you" might disappear. I'm talking about the parts of anxiety that as awful as they may have seemed, you eventually grew to understand. You grew to adapt to them, and maybe at some point, you even learned to love them. As a thirty-eight-year-old unmarried woman, I know exactly who I am today. Tomorrow may change, but for today, that's all that matters.

Before the birth of the Instabook, which has now become this awesome little book, I was in corporate America—not super corporate, since I was just working for a big-brand liquor company, but if there are benefits and a 401k, then that's corporate enough. Our company took on a new distributor, and new positions opened up, so I took the leap and tried it out, something I have always been excellent at in my career—personal life, not so much. So here I was, taking on a new role, a great pay raise, and a very long commute back to Long Island, where I once grew up. Long story short, I stayed in that position for 104 days. Yes, I counted; I have anxiety, remember. It was the wrong job for me. The actual description didn't do a very good job of clarifying what I would be getting into. It came with too high a learning curve for me to succeed, apart from all the other factors that weighed heavily too. So one Monday morning, I just quit. Was it that simple? Yes, it was. I didn't have to speak to anyone about the move I was going to make, because deep down in my gut, I knew this was right, and there was no anxiety about it. So just like that, I gave my three-weeks' notice. Because, c'mon now, I was still a professional and knew they were in a jam. Plus I didn't have any backup plan.

My entire life, I have had a backup plan for my backup plan, but since I was embracing all that I was and all that I'd achieved, I asked myself one very simple question: *Trish, what do you want?* The answer was already rooted somewhere inside me because I knew at some point that I would transition to being a full-time life coach and publish a book on anxiety. I just had no idea it was going to be now.

I have been coaching for over a decade. This had always been something I did on the side with very specific clients, due to my time constraints. So it was pretty simple for me to figure out that this would be my new path, my new venture in life. Let's not forget that this venture came with zero starting salary, no benefits, or anything else for that matter. Aha, so now I'm faced with a business challenge. Game on, let's do this. But first, let me check in with my anxiety—yep, all good there. So I continued on my new path. Right after I was done with my three weeks of salary life, I left for an already-booked trip to Hawaii with a group of friends. This trip was epic and life changing. It was Hawaii—of course it was epic. I was at the right place at the right time, with all the right people. Three rights can't make a wrong, or can they? Didn't matter, because it was all heading in the right direction.

While in Hawaii, we were chatting about what my next move was, what corporate job I was going to chase after now. I informed my friends of the coaching business I was interested in pursuing full-time and brought up the idea of writing about anxiety. It was then that my friend Jho mentioned he had this idea for an Instabook; mind you, this was not something that existed yet. He came up with this idea of writing a book on Instagram, kind of like a mini version of a book, made into posts so people could just read along whenever they wanted to. The idea was brilliant, and even more brilliant was the fact that Jho told me I was welcome to use the idea. All I had to do was just give credit where credit was due. So thank you, Jho. Also, in case you're wondering, yes, that's a nickname. His full name is Jose Antonio Hernandez.

That summer after I was unemployed, I decided just to travel and continue not having a plan. I still can't believe I did that, because my anxiety usually feels most comfortable with plans, deadlines, and hard facts to live by. I realized I could either live by my anxiety's terms or live through my anxiety, and that's what happened. I forced myself into an anxious state of living with no plan, no hard facts, just the knowledge that everything would eventually be okay. As you'll see through my journey in this book, the mere idea of the unknown would usually have sent me spiraling out of control. But now, anxiety no longer dictates my choices. Even as I write these pages, my life is still unknown because I'm an entrepreneur and that's just how things are.

I spent the next month visiting my family since they all live out of the country. Pie lives in Kaikoura, New Zealand, and my parents are now retired, living in Guatemala along with my very large extended family. I refer to my parents as the "Guates," mainly because I think it's a cute nickname and it's easier to say. The Instabook version of this book was born in New Zealand, which was fitting because of the severe panic attack I had suffered on the plane to New Zealand with my new bestie, Victor.

The main point of sharing my story with all of you is to get real about this disorder. I'm not trying to convince anyone that anxiety is curable; hell, if it were, then there wouldn't be any need for this book, right? What I do want people to know and understand is that even with severe anxiety/panic or any disorder, you can still live a very fulfilling and whole life. I push through all my difficult circumstances because what's the alternative? Let the disorder just take over? Most people who aren't in my inner circle were floored when they first started to read my Instabook. I don't blame them, because I never dared share anything about what I was going through. I mainly just suffered in silence. Plus, when I was growing up, mental illness was not something people discussed; it was more like something they looked down upon. I carried so much shame with me all these years because I thought something major must be wrong with me. How was everyone just functioning and carrying on like everything was normal when all I wanted to do was curl up in a ball and hide?

Those days are long gone now. I have made a career out of my dysfunction because it has given me my function as a life coach, speaker, and now author. Instead of suppressing my anxiety and white-knuckling it through life, I worked on myself, allowed myself to feel everything I needed to feel, and finally accepted the things that I can't change, like my anxiety. When I say work, I do mean work. You can't just change your perception overnight. Even coping skills have to be worked on. I'll go into more about the "work" under the treatments chapter.

Key Takeaways:

- Vulnerability lets people in.

- Anxiety is livable.

- Make friends on planes. They may become your mentors

Chapter 2

Where I Came From

"You are not a victim
Choose to be different
Choose to own your life
This is not a dress rehearsal
This is your reality
You are what you eat
You are what you speak
You are your world"

My parents came to this country at very young ages, having no education and unable to speak English. They were both born and raised in Guatemala, Central America (that's beneath Mexico, next to Belize, and above San Salvador). They left Guate to provide for their families back home. (Side note: Mom is one of nine kids, and Dad is one of five. The more kids people had back then the better their farms and businesses would be.) Neither one of my parents made it to high school, which I find so admirable because they have found a way to make their situations better rather than simply accepting the cards they were dealt. Mom came to NYC when she was just 18, working as a housekeeper for the uber rich on Park Avenue. Mom is our rock, I tell ya; they just don't make women like her. She will take on any obstacle head-on without looking back, regardless of whether she's qualified, scared, or ready. At her first job, she barely made four dollars an hour, but nevertheless, she took it, and that is how she met this woman I'll refer to as "Mrs. K." Mrs. K was married to Mr. K., and this man was about to change my mom's world forever.

Mr. K was an entrepreneur, and to be honest, I still have no idea what his exact title was. All I ever knew was that he was a very tall, distinguished man who lived in the Big House (more on that later, bear with me). So Mom started living with and working for the K's in their penthouse on the Upper East Side. Mom always went home for Christmas to visit her family, and that's where she met my playboy of a dad. Dad was the ultimate player, in soccer and love. He would love them and leave them, but once he saw my mom, he knew. I know, cute, right? Love does exist! But not according to him, because he's still a Latin man, so there's that machismo factor. Regardless, they connected, got married, and then got preggers.

My mom was worried about raising a child in the city; it wasn't what she wanted. Mr. K had purchased land in Locust Valley, Long Island. There was a mansion (aka the Big House), an apartment, and a cottage (aka the Little House). Mr. K offered to let the Guates move into the cottage rent-free to raise us and attend the school district there, which happened to be amazing. They happily accepted, and Mom became Mr. K's chef, and Dad became the landscaper. The property was fantastic, with a tennis court, a pool, an orchard, a rose garden, wild gardens, a greenhouse, etc. Apparently, I didn't know any better; growing up like this was my perspective of normal. I had my Jewish family, the K's, and my Guates. I was so happy and blessed.

For years, I never really knew the difference between rich and poor or anything about the middle class because my norm was distorted. Mr. K had four children, who were all much older than Pie and me; however, they still played with us whenever they came to the house. The kids went to boarding school, so we would see them only for the holidays and long weekends. Pie and I used to run around the Big House as if it was ours; that's just how Mr. K made us feel. He would be in his study, and I would run my little self in and ask him to play with me or watch me dance with my little pink radio at the time when I was apparently in love with Aretha Franklin (according to one of Mr. K's kids). Mr. K was not the warmest man, but when you're a little kid, you don't care who anyone is; you just want someone to pay attention to you and pick you up. My actions would mortify my mom. I would also write Mr. K these little handwritten notes about how much I loved him and asking him to visit me in the Little House. I know, tearjerker, right? Man, I was cute. I love the K's, and they will always be my family. They taught me how to play chess and tennis, and embrace ballet and the arts, but most importantly, they made me understand that race and religion do not define a family.

Everything sounds great, right? What a life—I was just living the childhood dream. This is where the record skips and everyone turns to say, "Why you messing with my groove, DJ?" My mom would always take us to Guatemala, which is a Third World country. My earliest memory is probably around seven or eight years old, when I started to comprehend that OMG, this is where I am from, not the rolling hills of Mr. K's gorgeous estate, where tennis whites were encouraged on the courts. *My actual family is quite poor—wait, so am I. Oh, so we're actually the help then. Does that mean the K's aren't my family?* I just didn't want to accept my actual reality, and because I was dealing with such a culture shock, the anxiety that followed was full blown. I started to question every aspect of my life. *Who am I? Where do I fit in? Who's my family?*

Mom would take us there for one month in the summer. I didn't exactly know what I was experiencing at first, but I did know that they were the most traumatic summers I ever had. I would be living in this constant state of anxiety, with panic attacks just coming and going whenever they pleased. Back then; no one spoke about anxiety disorder. I never even heard of it until my college years, in 1997. I was ridiculously skinny, and I have never had an eating disorder, but when your anxiety is that high, your metabolisms at super speed too, and you will burn through everything. I also didn't like feeling too full, because that would trigger the panic. (This still holds true today.) It makes me sad now to write this, but I loathed going to Guate. I would try to come up with any excuse I could find not to go. I refused to pack or let go of my dad when those days came. When I became more of a mouthy teen who rebelled, I simply said, "Nope, not going," and that was that. I was tired of the culture shock and the craziness that kept me a prisoner of my thoughts and body. To paint a more vivid picture, Guate back then didn't have paved roads, and electricity was scarce. Pie and I were taking baths in buckets—buckets, I say! We washed our clothes in a big *pilla* (a basin made of concrete, holding rainwater) that was made of stone and could rip a hole in even your toughest jeans. I wasn't able to appreciate the raw beauty that Guatemala held and, more so, what

12

my large family represented. Anxiety was able to strip this appreciation away from me for many years. I avoided Guate and never spoke to any of my 350 family members. It was disappointing for sure, but worse was that it wasn't that I didn't want to see them. It's just that I physically and mentally couldn't see them because my coping skills were failing me at all times.

Aside from this dual life I was living, what made things a bit more difficult was the language barrier between my parents and me. They weren't highly educated in the school system. They were more street-smart, which I can happily say I have picked up from them. Luckily, Pie is two years older, so she paved the way for all the explanations of exams, curfews, and what grounding was. Because I couldn't openly speak to my parents in a way that made them understand my needs, I felt like more of an outsider with anxiety disorder. Depersonalization was a constant in my younger years. Depersonalization can consist of reality or detachment within the self, regarding one's mind or body. You feel like you've changed, that the world has become vague, dreamlike, less real, or insignificant. This is a very disturbing experience, and when I said I didn't know who I was, this was the cause behind it. Have you ever looked in the mirror and not known who the hell was staring back at you?

During the younger years, Pie didn't know what was happening to me either. I hid my disorder very well. People would say, "Oh, she's just hyperactive, and eventually she'll gain weight and simmer down." Pie and I were the usual type of sisters. We fought, loved, and pretended the other didn't exist—ya know, normal teenage crap. We shared a room, which was helpful because I was always scared of the dark and hated sleeping alone. Pie was the polar opposite of me, which created a good balance between us. She loved to travel; she found it invigorating and exciting. I mean, for me, it was like a death sentence. I wanted things always to stay the same; I neither encouraged change nor wanted to be a part of it. She, however, embraced change and sought it out. She also kicked me out of her bed all the time, which I want to mention for no other purpose than to make her feel bad when she reads this. My reason for trying to sleep with everyone in the house was mainly because I was scared of my thoughts, and when you aren't able to articulate how you're feeling, the next best thing is to find a warm body and snuggle up with it. I don't recommend this as a coping skill; it's just that this was the only thing I could do to comfort myself at the time. There are so many amazing techniques now for dealing with night fears/terrors.

Another amazing medium for understanding and knowing more about anxiety disorder is through social media, which is now embracing mental awareness. There are now so many outlets available to get information from, simply at the touch of your fingertips. I never thought I would say this, but "back in my day," we didn't have Google, WebMD, cell phones, podcasts, etc. So if you wanted to know more about any subject, you would take yourself to a library, dig through a card catalog, and find a book that you couldn't sign out because of the fear of being embarrassed. So you sat in a corner, praying no one would find you reading about mental illnesses. The only reason I even majored in psychology was because I wanted to know what the hell was wrong with me! I was searching for answers; I guess I had been searching my whole life.

Key Takeaways:

- Travel is possible with anxiety.
- There is a plethora of info on mental illnesses.
- Depersonalization is a side effect of anxiety/panic disorder. Once treated for the other disorder, this side effect will diminish over time.

Chapter 3

When the Anxiety Started

"I'm not telling you it's going
to be easy
I'm also not telling you it
won't suck
But what I am telling you is
that it will be worth it"

My earliest memory of anxiety was around three or four years old, when kids go off to preschool. Because this was the first time I was away from my mom, I did what came naturally, which was to scream and kick anyone who was trying to separate us. Pie was in the same school, but that gave me zero comfort, for whatever reason. I saw the separation from my mom as impending doom—that I would never see her again, something awful would happen to her, and I wouldn't know because, dammit, we were separated. I get it, trust me. Looking back at that time in my life, I realize it was all quite irrational. But if you could be in my head at that exact moment, you would see that it was factual. No one could convince me otherwise. These were sure signs of separation anxiety; however, it just never got any easier, no matter what age. This is a good clue to look for because kids can grow out of separation anxiety when they realize everything is just how it was when they left their parents, and their brains form new synapses to send signals that all is okay in the world.

When entering a new grade with new teachers, or let's just say anything new, my world turned into turmoil. I just assumed everyone was like me and we just walked around not talking about it, so I never brought it up. I thought everyone had these levels of anxiety. Why didn't anyone tell me this was so abnormal?! Traveling to Guatemala certainly didn't help matters; it felt like some cruel test to see if I could survive.

I was that kid in school who got invited to a sleepover and was super excited, up until bedtime, when the lights were turned off, and then the panic set in and the dad had to come pick her up no matter what time it was. Now, one would think my parents would have forbidden me from sleeping anywhere, right? Nope! All they knew was that the phone would ring and Dad would get up to rescue his daughter. This even happened when I went out East to my friend's parents' house in the Hamptons (2.5 hours away from where we lived). I would be okay for most of the day, and then nightfall would come—now cue the panic. My parents never questioned me on this, and now that I think about it, it never even came up. There's a good reason why it never came up, and that is because Dad Barillas also suffers from anxiety, definitely inherited. Dad used to tell Pie and me that bad things would happen to us when we walked out the front door. He also hates traveling and suffers as much as I do on planes. I wish I knew this growing up; I would have felt so much less alone and ashamed. Mom always says that Dad and I are *son iguales*, which means we are two of the same, cut from the same cloth. This is quite true; we are so similar that it scares me sometimes. Dad never went to therapy, nor did he understand his anxiety, but that's okay. He's much older and from a different generation, and I help him whenever possible.

I recall a time in grade school when I did speak to one of my closest friends and tried my best to describe how I felt at times. She was a godsend. She probably doesn't remember a note she gave me that I've kept and used as a lifeline. She described my anxiety as "icky feelings," and the note she gave me was a list of everything I had to look forward to and be happy about. She was teaching me gratitude, and I am forever indebted to her. Thank you, Rebecca Gott. Apart from this piece of paper, there were other things significant to me too, like my pink radio and every Walkman and iPod that I've ever owned. Music was the other thing that gave me a sense of comfort. I would sleep with this pink radio playing under my pillow to soothe me. Again, I didn't know what I had. All I knew was that I had to try to do anything and everything to avoid the feelings.

So what were the feelings I was adamantly avoiding? I felt lost within my family. Unable to have clear, concise conversations with them, I was left frustrated and sad. I felt anxious all the time. Even in my sleep, I suffered from night terrors. I distracted myself. As a means of coping, I made sure I joined every club in school as well as sports. I was a super-active teenager, mainly because I was trying to outrun my anxiety. With anxiety can come panic attacks. There are two most-prominent versions of panic: the fear of losing control and the fear of having a heart attack. Mine is the fear of losing control.

Aside from the underlying anxiety always present in my day-to-day life, there would also be the panic attacks. They can start slowly or become a full-blown attack in seconds. For those with panic disorder, it's okay. Reading this doesn't mean you're going to have a panic attack—just breathe and continue. I say this because sometimes even reading literature on this disorder can induce a panic attack. What an oxymoron, right? The book to help you with your anxiety is giving you anxiety as you read it. I get it, trust me. I get it all too well, so let's keep pushing through. My panic brings on sweaty palms, an upset stomach, vomiting, trembling, depersonalization, catastrophic thoughts, and "what if" thinking. It's hard to articulate the exact thoughts. It's like trying to describe what being drunk feels like to someone who has never had a drink in his or her life. A good comparison is when you first get on a roller coaster—that anxiety you feel as the roller coaster is ticking upward, right before it drops. You feel short of breath, with racing thoughts and sweaty palms, and you just want to make it over that hill so your anxiety goes away. However, you're not on a ride, and that's what scares you the most, because now how the hell do you get off? Where's your sense of relief?

When I'm spiraling, I think that I have some horrible sickness and that the nausea may never go away, so I'll have to live this way forever. I also can't process my thoughts slowly; they're going a hundred miles a minute. My breathing is shallow, and I start rubbing my palms up and down my thighs. I think to myself, *why is this happening again? What's wrong with me?* I start to question my mental stability and whether I'm just going to snap and start running around like a crazy person or faint and never wake again. Deep breaths, for my anxiety peeps. It's okay. You're okay. And we can all live with and through this. So the positive is that when in a high state of panic, your adrenaline can only spike for fifteen minutes or so, and then it comes back down. What's happening is the fight-or-flight response, which evolved as a survival technique, but somehow we got it misdirected as a way to respond to our anxiety.

One technique that I will highlight here is to let the anxiety/panic happen. Easier said than done, I know. Trust me, I hear ya. But it's something you need to practice to make it a habit, right? So when you feel anxious, just go with it. Feel the anxiety, and keep on doing whatever you're doing. Regarding panic, this tends to be a bit more difficult, but don't try to deny what's happening, because the more you push it away the stronger it's going to get. Accepting what's happening takes power away from the anxiety. There have been numerous times I've just sat there shaking in front of people, and I didn't try to wish it away. I just said, yes, well this is happening. And believe me, it seemed to last a much shorter time than all the other times this had popped up. Is it embarrassing? Sure. But then again, so is being overly intoxicated, and we've seen—or been—those people a few times in our lives, and we all survived those episodes. See, so it's the same thing. Don't be ashamed of something that is physically or mentally happening. No one is perfect, and we all suffer on some level. I am very open and honest about my disorder now, as someone who for a good thirty years was ashamed and lived in fear that people would find out and judge her.

If I try to pinpoint how the anxiety started for me really, it comes down to a combination of several things. For starters, I inherited it from my dad. My upbringing was far from normal, and throwing in the cultural shock at such a young age was the perfect recipe for anxiety to move in and take up residence in my head. My central nervous system is quite sensitive and directly correlates with my digestive system. The digestive piece is significant because most people don't realize that what they eat and how they digest it can factor into how much anxiety they experience. The fight-or-flight response takes up a lot of your brain's resources, so to compensate, it slows down parts of your brain that aren't as necessary, such as the muscles involved in digestion. Normally, since the fight-or-flight response is only supposed to be temporary, you would never notice that your digestion has changed. But because anxiety is a constant, long-term, chronic issue, you're left with a digestive tract that isn't running correctly. That can cause several different issues, but of course, it often leads to constipation, diarrhea, gas, bloating, and traditional indigestion.

Similarly, the same neurotransmitters in your brain that are altered and affect your mood, like serotonin, also play a role in sending signals to the gut. While low serotonin can cause anxiety, anxiety can also cause low serotonin. That means some of the messengers that are normally traveling through your body are possibly being created at a lower rate, leading to digestion issues.

Another issue relates to adrenaline. During the fight-or-flight response, your body creates massive amounts of adrenaline to give you extra energy. To do that, adrenaline needs to take the energy from "sugar storage"—places in your body that store sugars that can be turned into a nutrient known as glycogen. While adrenaline does this, your body starts essentially processing nutrients at rates that aren't ideal. It also changes how your body processes nutrients and could conceivably affect your digestive health.

Inside your intestines are bacteria, both good and bad. Most bacteria are "good bacteria," and they are designed to help you digest food and improve your overall health. But these bacteria need to be in the right balance. Good bacteria are constantly battling against bad bacteria, and in some cases, the bad bacteria can win. Furthermore, good bacteria are only "good" when they're kept in check by other good bacteria. If something happens to cause any bacterial overgrowth, it can hurt the strength of your stomach. For reasons that aren't entirely clear but most likely have something to do with the way anxiety weakens the immune system, bacterial balance inside the intestines seems to be affected by stress. Those who experience long-term anxiety may have improperly balanced bacteria that are not digesting food correctly, ultimately causing digestion problems.

It's important to listen to your body; to the signals it gives you. I had no idea that these all tied up together with my digestive problems. As soon as I realized this—or shall I say, as soon as I was hospitalized for many medical ailments—I started to pay close attention. I found myself a homeopathic doctor, who ran every test under the sun to see what my body was able to process and digest, as well as finding out what my body was deficient in. I always assumed I was somewhat healthy, even with all the anxiety; I was fit and getting enough sleep. I chalked up my sensitive stomach to something I always had or got stuck with, like a birthmark or something. My thought process was, *oh, that stomach again, grrr.*

Wish I was born with a stronger system. No, Trish, just change your eating habits and take the right supplements. After I had the right doctors and the right tests, I soon started my supplements, and within two months, my energy, digestion, and all-around mental health vastly improved.

Key Takeaways:

- Don't fight off anxiety. Let it happen.

- Pay attention to your digestive track. Is it is trying to tell you something?

- Anxiety can be hereditary. Have you asked anyone in your family if they suffer from this disorder as well?

Chapter 4

Transitional Points in My Life

"I don't know what normal is
I don't want to ever find out
I do what's natural
I speak my truth
I choose my life over anyone else's
I choose me"

This is where the anxiety plays such a significant role in my life. I sometimes wonder where I may have ended up if I never had this disorder. But then I remind myself that I am exactly where I should be and I would have ended up at the same place regardless. The transition to college was beyond brutal. I wasn't ready to leave my family and friends, nor did I understand the disorder fully, so I was unprepared. I applied to eleven colleges and got into ten of the eleven. Thanks a lot, UPenn. No worries though, I don't hold grudges.

Why would someone apply to eleven colleges? Well, funny you should ask. Deep down, I didn't want to leave the comfort of my hometown or my parents. Anxiety made me a creature of habit; I needed order at all times, no surprises. Moving to another state with people I had never met sent me into this crazy anxiety hole. This hole I speak of is the one where you're anxious every single second of every single day. Should someone so much as even breathe in my direction, I would jump out of my skin because I was so on edge and super high-strung all the time. One by one, my friends would leave for college. I felt as if I was experiencing a death, but this is where I started to understand that no, not everyone was wired like me, because my friends were so excited to be starting these new chapters in their lives. They were embracing the change, and meeting new people was just the bonus. I chose to go to a school in Massachusetts, which was a good 4.5 hours away but only 1.5 hour from my sis. How I chose this particular school should have been a tip-off. I tend to err on the side of minor OCD tendencies.

The school I had looked at and chosen was renovated. The freshman dorms were literally brand new, which meant I would be the first person to use the room, along with my assigned roommate. Who chooses a school based on cleanliness? That would be me. Leaving my parents was horrific, definitely in the top-four saddest moments of my life. Because my parents are foreign and didn't understand the legal age limits of anything, I was able to do whatever I chose to do as long as I respected them and myself. My parents were so cool with me that they didn't meddle into any of my social issues and just let me be. Leaving them felt wrong because, let's not forget, I have severe separation anxiety, especially when it comes to my dad. Yep, I'm a daddy's girl.

I lasted a whole four months at WNEC, my college in Massachusetts. I had to call my dad and tell him I hated it, and I think he just left the phone dangling (yes, the era of house lines). He got in the car to come collect me. I was severely underweight because anything I ate couldn't stick. The anxiety was in full swing, even working overtime. I barely understood anything in class. I spent the entire time having depersonalization episodes with bouts of panic. Everyone and everything seemed so out of sync, with people I couldn't relate to all around me. I felt as if I had been drugged and was just floating in and out of reality. Luckily, my boyfriend—we'll refer to him as "BF-A"—was with me at college, but I still chose to leave because I knew something was drastically wrong and I was fearful of my life.

I came home for a semester and attended a college in my hometown, not one that I was going to stay at; it was simply for the interim. Pie went to school in Connecticut, so I did what seemed logical and transferred to her school. The panic and anxiety became worse with every single day. My poor boyfriend, whom I dated all four years of college, was super supportive and would visit me no matter where I was. At this point, I was 5'2" and weighed seventy-eight pounds. I was having bouts of fainting spells because my body was becoming so weak. Once again, I called my dad and told him something was wrong and I needed to come home. For him, this was the best news ever because, due to his anxiety, he liked having me close to home or living under the same roof. I packed up my things for the second time and tried to tell myself everything was going to be okay, but I needed to look into my mental health because I was slipping into a version of myself that I didn't recognize.

Here I was again, being sent back to my parents with a severe nutritional problem. My parents didn't know what was wrong with me or where to send me. I went to a treatment center for eating disorders. The only issue was that I didn't have an eating disorder. I ate all the time, but nothing stuck. Some people would say, "You poor thing, what an awful problem to have," with a sarcastic undertone while rolling their eyes. I know it's a hard concept to grasp for those who battle with being overweight, but it's the same mental stress for those who can't gain weight, or at least it was for me. Being too thin was embarrassing. Nothing fit me. I felt tired all the time. And the one thing everyone did was pass judgment. Anxiety is a tricky disorder because I was so high-strung that my metabolism was at super speed. Nothing was slowing that bad boy down.

I stopped going to the treatment center when one of the nutritionists recommended I smoke weed. It was 1999. Clearly, weed wasn't legal, and if anyone knows panic attacks, this was a sure way to end up in the hospital. Again, I'm not pretending to be some innocent little thing. I did my fair share of experimenting with drugs before anxiety moved into my headspace. Someone mentioned that I should try acupuncture at the New York College of Acupuncture in Long Island. I went, and it started to help with my digestion and calm the anxiety to a degree. I'll get into this later on in the "Treatments" chapter, as there were many I tried.

While at home, I had time to do some serious self-reflecting. I have always been a night person, unable to ever fall asleep at a reasonable hour. So one night, it happened. There was an infomercial (our version of marketing on a media platform back then) airing late, around 2:30 a.m. It started off with, "Do you suffer from x, y and z" What they began to describe was an anxiety disorder. My eyes were glued to the TV. I was almost in tears to hear someone speak about everything that was happening to my body and mind. I leapt from my bed, ran into my parents' room, and declared, "I have an anxiety disorder." I must have said it a million times before my dad asked if I was on drugs or drunk. They eventually kicked me out of their room, but I could barely sleep knowing there was a name for my disorder. I then called some people I knew and trusted with my life and asked if they'd heard of this so-called "anxiety disorder." One of my girlfriends said, "Yeah, I know a girl who sees an anxiety specialist." *Wait, what, there are anxiety specialists out there in the world, and I haven't seen one yet?* Well let me tell you, this news was earth-shattering. It was like someone just freed me of the weights that had been placed on my wrists, and ankles: finally free of the shackles.

As soon as humanly possible, I was sitting with an anxiety specialist, discussing my panic attacks. He had a plethora of information, and soon I had every workbook, textbook, and brochure on the disorder. I was a psychology major, but we hadn't yet gone into this territory, so I was well ahead of the game. I spent more of my waking hours reading all about my disorder than doing my actual college work. There was a point during my recovery from this disorder where I started to become a bit agoraphobic (fear of leaving your home). When you dive into therapy, it gets harder before it gets better. Just reading about my disorder would trigger the anxiety. I was becoming scared to be or do anything by myself. My college boyfriend would have to come over late at night or stay over because I didn't want to be alone with my thoughts. I honestly don't know how he was so patient with me, but I know he saw the struggle. And even though he never quite understood it, he never for one second made me feel ashamed. The disorder ruined quite a few of my relationships because I didn't embrace or know who I truly was yet. I didn't know my power or the value that I added to anything or anyone. This is described in more detail in the "Relationships" chapter. So here I am, learning about anxiety and still living in anxiety. It was all so complicated, but I managed to gain some weight back—acupuncture was helping with my digestion—and was beginning to focus on my studies finally.

I do want to point out that even though I was speaking to a specialist, it didn't correct my previous behavior and coping skills. I was still in my pattern of packing my schedule so that anxiety had no time to creep in. I made plans so far in advance with everyone so that I knew my time would be filled up and I never had to be alone with myself and process all that had happened. Since I had transferred so many times, I had to take the maximum amount of credits and was working two part-time jobs. It's exhausting just thinking about it. Miraculously, I ended up graduating college on time—well, more like I was able to walk with my graduating class and took an independent study elsewhere to receive my diploma. I had started bartending at a restaurant/bar during the last year of college and realized I could make so much more money as a bartender than at my other jobs. This was the start of something epic, but I didn't know it then.

I stayed with my BF-A for the full four years of college, up until my last semester. He and I both needed to make up credits due to our transfers. I will never forget that year. It was New Year's

2000, the millennial. Things didn't go as planned. BF-A broke up with me, and I broke my tailbone, nose, and collarbone while out on NY's Eve. I was pushed off a stage when security started to spray down the crowd as the ball dropped, and I had nothing to cushion my fall. This started one of the worst years of my life. I had to cope with my accident, missing an entire semester of college, and the heartbreak of my first love. You know the one, where you feel like you don't have air to breathe in because you lost part of your lungs. Nothing was comforting. I was so codependent that my world shattered when BF-A left me. I walked around as if some of my limbs were missing. I was a tragedy. Anxiety turned into depression. I don't recall much of this period, because I'm pretty sure I blocked that time span. I used so much of my time focusing on BF-A to avoid all the anxiety that was plaguing me. So I did what anyone else with such a disorder would do: I got a new boyfriend and two other jobs while taking twenty-one credits—avoid, avoid, avoid.

I worked part-time at a local bar. The owner was such a kind man; he almost felt like a second father to me. Let's just say, I was hanging out with people and doing things that could have seriously changed the course of my life. I was one of the only women who worked at the bar, because you had to be your barback and this required tons of physical labor. He generally only hired guys. Well this 5'2" Latina wasn't going to let that happen. Present me with a challenge, and I'll happily accept. Not only will I accept it, but I will go above and beyond to be an overachiever.

After I graduated college, I went through some personal trauma. I was roofied while attending a college formal with a guy from some fraternity. I had a feeling I shouldn't have accepted the invite, but I did, and off I went. I knew I was in a bad situation when I was sitting in a bus, unable to move my body, and yet my thoughts were crystal clear. I somehow managed to drag myself to the bus driver, and they dropped me off on the sidewalk of a hospital in a town far from where I lived. Thank God Pie was still living at my parents' house at the time, because she picked up the phone and came to get me. That night in the hospital was horrific; I could feel the poison in my body. I was tied down to the bed because I was convulsing due to my anxiety disorder. I also had no health insurance, so they placed me in the drug ward. I have never been so happy to see my sister because, fu*k man, I was scared to death.

I had to work the next day at the bar, and it only took five minutes for the owner to come over and ask me what the hell happened. Then he fired me. He didn't fire me for being a bad employee. He fired me because he cared deeply about my life and my future. He didn't have daughters of his own, just sons. He sat me down and said, "I have to let you go for your own good. You need to get out of here, and not this bar but this town." He proceeded to say that he saw so much potential in me and that staying in one place may not be the best because I needed to grow and explore other avenues of life. He said, "Don't let your mind limit what you have the potential to do." To this day, that was one of the most impactful talks I've ever had. I left right after our talk and never worked another day there again.

A month later, I moved in with my high school friend in the city, the one I swore I would never move to. This seems to be a pattern of mine. Whenever I swear, "I would never," I do exactly that but a few years later. So there it was, a series of bad events leading up to moving to the city I now love with every fiber of my being. I felt like my move was almost a rebirth to reclaim my life from anxiety. This was another epic turning point; I was so ready for more out of life. Due to all my moving around during college, my parents were pretty much banking on the fact that maybe I'd just stay for six months and then return home. My move was one thing that I did with no hesitation or second guesses; it just felt right in my gut. I chose NYC because, in complete honesty, my dad wouldn't allow me to go much farther (insert his anxiety right here).

My high school guy friends all picked someone to live with, and we made sure we lived close to each other. Funny enough, during this giant move to NYC, I had zero anxiety. My body had the opposite reaction; I was happy to be among the chaos, with the hustle and noise of the city that never sleeps. I found a place that understood me, a city I was able to call home and grow into. My first years were truly epic. I found a job that silenced any anxiety. Hell, it could take out your whole memory if you let it.

Key Takeaways:

- There are anxiety specialists.

- Don't force things to happen.

- Invest in your mental health always.

Chapter 5

Careers

"Bet on yourself

the house never loses"

So here I am in the Big Apple, where dreams are made or shattered. I would say I'm just now coming into "living the dream," which is this exact moment in time. While I was finishing an independent study in the South Bronx and living on the Upper East Side in my soapbox apartment, I needed money—and not just some money, like real money to pay my bills. The guy I was dating mentioned a nightclub he went to and suggested I get a job there. This was such a pivotal point in my life because it was at this club that I met so many people who basically aided in my future career that led to many job endeavors. I walked into this club and asked for a manager. They didn't even have an opening; I just went on a whim and took a chance. The manager happened to be there, so I bounced inside and sat with him. I didn't feel the discrimination against short people until I went into nightlife. To be honest, I didn't even know I was that short. So as I gave my crappy resume with no mentionable bar experience, he scanned me up and down with a grin on his face, which wasn't because he liked what he saw. It was more like a look that said, "What the hell is this little girl doing?" Not only am I vertically challenged at 5'2", but I don't look that old either.

I have always had great genes from the Guates and tend to look younger than I am, so I was just a little girl standing in a nightclub. I never saw this as an issue going into the job world and whatnot, but wow, for sure, this is a thing. And clearly, they don't mention how hiring for certain positions also means certain height requirements. This guy was drilling me with all sorts of questions, mainly about how I would handle their volume if I had never done it before. My reply was no different than my personality: "Just try me." I had this air of confidence about me that I could do anything. I think battling anxiety just sucked so much that I thought, *how hard could bartending be?* My dad also had me believing that I could do anything. He was so supportive, and I created this quite badass attitude about myself—yes, and a bit cocky too.

It's so crazy to have almost two different egos in the same body, but it happens. On the one hand, I had the ego that I could do anything: "Step out da way!" Then when anxiety would creep in, it would be, "I'm petrified of my thoughts and body." So, as you see, I was in a constant seesaw of thoughts and battles, but it was all against myself, my inner thoughts that I had at some point created in my head. It isn't something you can even describe to someone if they haven't experienced it themselves. It goes back to my example of describing being drunk to someone who has never taken a sip of alcohol. You can never recreate the experience until you have gone through it. Going through the transitions in my life has now let me create the mental balance that I was so desperately seeking.

Ok, so back to the nightclub interview. I think for his viewing pleasure, he said, "Okay, come in on Friday. You'll work from 12:00

a.m. to 2:00 a.m.," which was the busiest time of the club, and mind you, this was right when bottle service had arrived on the scene, so there were only a few paying tables, and everyone else had to grab drinks from the bar. I wasn't getting paid or making tips. It was just to see if I could handle the crowd and make the club money. I had to fight the other veterans to prove myself. Hey, if I were that guy, I would have found it highly entertaining as well. So here I was, twenty-one years old, fighting for space at a club and flying around the bar at full speed. I left after 2:00 a.m. and cried the whole way home, realizing how out of place I was, and vowed never to even walk down that street EVER again. Next morning, I got a call from the manager. Apparently, I killed it, and he said, "Congrats, you get the crap shifts. You want them or not?" Hell yeah, I took it, and well, the rest is history. I stayed in nightlife for 13.5 years, and the manager became one of my closest friends and looked after me during my early stages of NYC innocence.

While I was working all the crap shifts at my first nightclub, I also worked during the day at Lord & Taylor, in the advertising department. If you've ever seen the movie *Sliding Doors*, this would have been one of those transitional points. I wasn't in grad school yet, and I was just trying out all these new ventures for a bit before I committed to another several years of schooling. Since I was so young, sleep never really crossed my mind, and I was all about the hustle. Let's just say that bartending two nights at the nightclub was better for me financially than my two-week paycheck. I knew I was only twenty-one years old and needed to start at the bottom, but at that time, it just wasn't an option for me. My parents were in a tough spot, and I had to try to figure out how to pay rent, pay for school, and help out the parents, so here came the sliding doors. After six months at L&T, I was offered a 30 percent raise and an office—no window, but c'mon, still an office. (P.S. I was making peanuts, so trust me, this wasn't a dream offer.) The woman who made the offer was floored when I declined. She even commented that I was chasing a fast life that was just unrealistic. What was real to me was paying bills and striving to be more authentic and different. The average nine-to-five was never my road map. I knew this at a young age, and my anxiety also ran rampant back then, so physical exertion was necessary. Realistically, nightlife was exactly what I needed at that exact point in my life.

Nightlife was different back then; it was based on who you knew and how interesting you were, not so much on the expense accounts, the suits, or DJs that cost more than people make in an entire year, just to play for two hours. I loved nightlife back then; it was my savior, for both my financial needs and, without knowing it, my anxiety. Sometimes I realize that my anxiety behaves much like a sheepdog: If it's cooped up all day, it will act out and perhaps destroy your home. My body worked quite similarly: I needed to exert my energy to get rid of my anxiety. Bartending in a slammed nightclub is both physically and mentally taxing. It was perfect. Most of those years that I worked crazy hours and double shifts and went to school, I didn't experience much anxiety at all. To be honest, I assumed it went away until my then boyfriend—we'll call him BF-B—planned long vacations. And once I was pulled away from the nonstop work and was made to sit still, it all came back in full force. I know I stayed in nightlife longer than needed because, well seriously, the money was just incomparable to anything I would ever make at that age, or possibly ever (before it went corporate and before the audits happened).

Even though my height seemed to always come up at each venue where I worked, we traveled as a pack with my first manager. Whenever he left to open a new "hot spot," we always came as the openers. It was a handful of bartenders, cocktail waitresses, and bussers that made up this "A-Team." I was definitely by far the youngest at that point, and I was just trying to hustle and get my life going as soon as possible. I was so young at twenty-two years old, making bank (lots of money), and everything was paid in cash—tips were cash, and our payouts were cash. Those were the "cash is king" days. I made more money in those years than I ever have, and I'm not sure I can come close to those figures ever again, just so you guys can get an idea of why I stayed in it for so long. For the record, this cannot be held against me in a court of law, as I am an honest taxpayer. Anyway, it was at the height of the bottle-club era, and I happened to be at the right place at the right time, with the right people. Not gonna lie, I was a pretty damn fast bartender who always worked both the service and regular bar—my hospitality peeps will understand what that means. I was flying around the bar at super speed, nonstop. When a new place would open and the owners would question why someone my size was hired, my manager would say, "She's the best service bartender you could have. Watch her for a night and you'll see."

This apparently went on for years, and people began to know my name and my talent at tending bar, so I went on to work at all the top nightclubs in NYC. I did find a home at one company that

I stayed with for years. That's where I became a bar manager and then floor manager, and I was being groomed for GM but never got that far, as I was ready to take on a new venture by the time that opportunity came around. Those years were so goddamn amazing. Before the crash of 2008, I just assumed this type of money would always be around and just worked my freakin' ass off. Anxiety . . . what was that? Anxiety never came around because there wasn't a minute to spare for it. I lived with my BF-B, and we worked together, so life as I knew it was perfect. I was in love, raking in money and planning for a future that was never going to become a reality—well, not just then anyway. It was at this one particular nightclub that I made most, if not all, of my best friends. This nightclub was special. It just created such a loving space of dysfunction that functioned. Oxymoron, yes, but I don't care—it's my book. My BF-B and I ran it for several years, keeping much of the original staff, and it just felt like a family, one big crazy family.

The next massive transition happened when BF-B and I broke up. This wasn't just losing a relationship; this was losing my home, which I loved, and a job that I loved even more. Most people pass judgment on those who work in nightlife, and I say, let them. Nightlife is different. It's made for certain people, just like anything else in life. To end a relationship that wasn't serving me anymore was devastating. I lost most of myself. Some of those pieces I won't ever be able to get back, and over the years, I have made my peace with that. Rebuilding my life meant starting over. I wish I were able to break up with my anxiety, but nope, we're pretty much married for the long haul.

I don't want to skip over all the other career ventures I had during this time of exploration in nightlife. So here they are. I did an independent study in South Bronx as a play therapist in a treatment center for abused children. This was tough for me, mentally, but I needed it for the credits to receive my diploma, and it taught me that I was unable to become a social worker. I then enrolled at City College of New York to pursue a degree in landscape architecture. Apparently biology isn't my thing and seems as though that's a big piece of the curriculum. Then I signed up to take my LSAT and took a yearlong course to apply to Fordham Law School to become a divorce attorney. Once I saw the syllabus and the projected three-year plan and was told that I wouldn't be able to work a job, well then, that went out the window. I also bombed the LSAT because I let my ego get in the way, so I doubt Fordham would have even taken me. Finally, I saw a life coach who, I'm happy to say, has become one of my mentors, and he was all I needed. I knew right then that I wanted to become a life coach. So I enrolled at NYU, and sure enough, I had found my calling. It appealed to me on every level; nothing was wrong with this one. The nightclub I worked at let me do some of my organizational coaching requirements on their staff, so it was a win-win for me. Trust me, this was over a span of two years, but by 2006, I was a certified life personal and career coach. That decision gave me no anxiety, no weird gut reaction, which is usually how I can tell if something's good for me or not. I try to see if it speaks to my inner truth.

Even though I got certified as a life coach in 2006, I was too scared to let go of my crazy, noisy, and exhausting nightlife career because I knew that as soon as things slowed down, the anxiety would come creeping back in like a stubborn ex. Toward the end of my nightlife career, I just knew it was over for me. I was getting too old for those hours, and I started to become an angry person, where if you looked at me, you would just go, "Wow, get a new job, 'cause you're miserable." I wasn't able to hide it anymore, so the end of my long-term relationship became a push toward a different path.

I left my safe space at the club and went to open a hotel, thinking it would be calmer and have more normal hours. Yeah, no idea what I was thinking. You have no idea what a bloody nightmare opening a hotel is. It's no joke. It's open 24/7, and there are issues every second of every day. The company I was working for didn't have the correct staffing, so I became everything: payroll, BOH, FOH, floor manager—you name it, and I did it. This only lasted less than six months because, once again, I was losing so much weight, not eating, and even developing two ulcers in my small intestine. Safe to say, I was beyond stressed, so I quit without another job and went to visit my sis in New Zealand for several weeks.

While I was away, a big alcohol company called me and said they wanted to interview me. They even said they would wait the several weeks I was overseas. I thought they were joking and would have filled the position by the time I got back, but as luck would have it, they waited for me and were most eager to meet me. I didn't know anything about the position they were offering, but I did know that this company needed a female with a degree. Not only did I have a degree, but also two in fact. Plus I had been in hospitality my entire career, so why the hell not? At the same time, I also got another offer from a previous employer for a job with more managing, but something told me to take on this new venture with the alcohol company. So that's exactly what I did. However, I knew I finally had to deal with this whole anxiety issue, so here it was, the time of reckoning.

The week I started my new corporate alcohol job, it was so overwhelming that I had to convince myself not to quit every day, literally every day. The thing about going from a crazy nightlife environment to a quiet, normal-hour, day job was the slowness. Let me try to explain. In the nightlife, I was pulled in a million different directions: fix this; speak to this angry customer; we have a flood; the ice machine broke—you get the idea. Every second of the night was consumed with putting out fires, and it exhausted my brain as well as my body, which worked great for my anxiety, or so I thought.

Working for this new company, there was a lot of downtime, going from account to account, and waiting for people to get back to you. I was also working from home, so this was all so new and different to me. I knew the job wasn't going to be the issue; the issue was staying in it, because my instinct was to flee and run back to my comfort zone. I hired a therapist and told her that her only job was to keep me in mine. This scenario was what I had avoided my entire life—being flooded with thoughts, not having a home base, and working with no structure and no control of my days. My poor bestie, I had to stay at her apartment many a night because the panic got so bad before I went to sleep. But eventually, this slowness became my new norm, and I started to acclimate my entire life to this norm. I wasn't a big fan of the therapist. She did do her job correctly enough, though, because I stayed with the company for five years. There were tons of ups and downs, and not a single person knew how difficult it was for me to act normal and remain cool on the outside while I was dying on the inside.

As much as it pains me to say this, it took me close to a year to get over the initial anxiety of this new lifestyle. The job itself was great. It was in an industry I had been in my whole life, with people I had known and grown close to. So, seriously, this was a layup regarding job transitions. But that doesn't change the fact that it took a lot of adjusting to get used to it. Even going to sleep at night without my phone blowing up was unsettling. I went from feeling like a trauma surgeon that was on call for over thirteen years to being in retirement. My brain could not compute at all why I now felt unneeded, and what was I to do now with all this energy I had bottled up inside me? Going back to my sheepdog analogy, I wasn't being worked enough, and now I was gnawing off my leg in desperation.

Therapy, combined with acupuncture and lots of exercises, was what helped me through, along with anti-anxiety meds. The other part of my job that was spiking my anxiety was that I never had a home base other than working out of my apartment the days when I had to catch up on admin work. My line of work had me all over Manhattan, BK, Queens, and Staten Island. For those of you who are like me; need to be familiar with your surroundings, this was as horrible as it sounds. I liked going to one place every day; it was comfortable and gave me some form of structure. Not with this job though, every day was different. There was zero sense of any structure, and I could be all over the five boroughs within one day, so it pushed my boundaries, both literally and figuratively.

Looking back now, this was one of the best career decisions I had ever made, because when you're really pushed out of your comfort zone, you start to realize all the crap you can actually do when you need to. It's like finding out you have all this potential to be great that you never even knew existed. I had some great coworkers too, so that always helps. And I don't just mean professional, hardworking coworkers; I mean the kind you like and can hang with. I'm not trying to be PC. We were all just a bunch of really funny, down-to-earth, cool people. You would want to hang with us, I promise. So my job came down to negotiating for our brands with nightclubs, restaurants, and hotels. It was one of the best gigs out there. It was so social, and we had to know what's new, what's happening, and what's trending, so this was just my domain.

I remember, when I was in nightlife, on my way to work, I would be admiring all the people who were sitting in restaurants, chatting with friends and clients after work. For years, my life didn't have that. I worked six nights a week, so there weren't any dinners, birthdays, or weddings that I went to, because I was always working, and I needed the money, so I barely took off. You know how they say, "Be careful what you wish for." Yep, well, when I started at this new job, all I ever did was entertain my friends and clients, and go to dinners, lunches, drinks, etc. I would secretly laugh to myself because I knew I asked for this, and here I was with exactly what I wanted, and—plot twist—I was exhausted. Life is all about moderation, but when it's your job to be seen out and about, and to take people out and make deals, man, it really tainted the experience for me. Not because I didn't love it, trust me, I still do love it, but it was just so often, and I was getting burnt out real fast. But through it all, I started to realize what I wanted out of my life and my job. By slowing things down, I was able to think clearly and put things in perspective.

I have been offered many jobs to relocate, some within the US and some out of the country. For those of us who have my type of anxiety, you can't help but laugh at yourself when people ask this. I don't laugh because it's humorous; I laugh because it's so ironic that someone is asking me to take a job somewhere else, in some location I'm not familiar with. It would be a miracle if I were even to travel there, let alone conduct actual business and function normally there! I know life would be very different for me had I been able to get up and move, but c'mon! I transferred four times in college because that was too hard for me to handle. I never had to travel for work until I started my former job, which, to be honest, wasn't that bad. We traveled maybe three to four times a year, and I managed it, or at least I managed it to a certain degree. There did come a time while we were traveling when I was told that if my anxiety was that big an issue, then I should seriously consider a different career. Mind you, I had been in that job for over five years, so this came as a complete shock, and that is when I felt like my personal life and mental health should never be used against me. It made me sick to hear it. I have pretty thick skin when it comes to business, and I always conduct myself in a very professional manner, but this comment shattered me. I'm not sure why people think making such bold statements regarding mental health is okay, because it sure as hell is not. Luckily for me, the Universe corrected the situation; we were both placed on different work platforms and no longer needed to ever work together again. The situation solved itself, but this could have been a really big deal for me, and I may have had to leave sooner than I did. My anxiety never came up again because, well, why would it? In all my years of working, this was the only isolated incident. Sometimes people just aren't aware of the magnitude of certain mental health issues. Just because you may look or act a certain way, people assume you're trying to make things up, when all you've really been doing the whole time is trying to remain cool, calm, and collected so no one would even know that you have a disorder.

I was coming up on my fifth year when our company changed distributors, and that's when I saw an opportunity for a job change and new venture. My mentor at the time happened to be the president of the entire alcohol company, so yeah, that helped. All about who ya know, right? He strongly suggested I make a move. So up and off I went. The funny part of this experience was the fact that I now had to do the reverse commute from NYC to Long Island, basically back to where I grew up. This job seemed more in line with what I wanted to do, or so I thought. This was a new division/undertaking for the distributor, so it was new territory for everyone. At first, the commute would give me anxiety because I had to take a train 1.5 hours to my office, and I was always worried I would miss the train or we would get delayed or stuck. Plus, as an anxiety sufferer, being in control plays a huge role in whether or not you feel comfortable. I prefer to stay close to home, or close enough that it'll come down to only a fifteen-to-twenty-minute cab ride should I need to get back to my safe space. Not with this new job though. Normally, I never would have even considered taking the job, but my career outweighed my need to be comfortable. Sometimes in life, you just have to take that leap and remember that no matter what happens, at least it will always be a learning experience.

So here I was, commuting. I got the salary I requested and a lot more too; everything was nicely bundled into my contract. So, 104 days into my new job, I gave my notice. There are soooooooooo many reasons why this happened: the job description wasn't anywhere near accurate; my learning curve was far too extensive; and my director, whom I reported to, was unhappy with me as a hire in general. I was fighting a fight I knew I wasn't going to win. I definitely had inner battles with myself about staying or leaving. This led me to have anxious dreams at night, night terrors, or barely let me sleep at all. I knew something was wrong, but this time I knew the difference between anxiety and just being displaced, and that was what I was: displaced. I loved so many of my coworkers. They were the sweetest, hardest-working group of people I've had the pleasure of working with. I know 104 days is like the blink of an eye, but it was during these 104 days that I learned the most.

I connected so quickly with everyone at work, and I always seemed to have an office full of people who needed to chat more about life than about our crazy work organization. The more I sat on the train, in the stillness, the more I started to realize what was important in my life. Was it the money I was making, the clothes I could buy, and the title I was striving for, or was it for the balance in my life, helping others, and having the ability to travel and see my family whenever I wanted?

In this new position, I was busting my ass, trying to learn as much as possible, squish it all into my brain, and still find time to sleep. Forget my social life; it was diminishing before my eyes. I could barely respond to texts. No way did I make it to any events, and forget the weekends. They were jam-packed with either taking the Excel classes I needed or decompressing. If you notice in the previous sentences, everything was coming from a place of "I," which is all ego-based. The second portion that was really important regarding balance was my true authentic self. I knew deep down in my gut that this wasn't the right fit for me, and don't even get me started on some aspects of my director. It was clear from the get-go that we were not going to vibe and I was going to get buried. At the end of one particular workweek, I realized I was losing self-confidence and belief in myself. I can handle many situations. You can take my job, my money, even my home, but the moment you start to chip away my self-worth, that's my breaking point.

You know those decisions you make without having to consult anyone on? Those gut decisions where it doesn't matter if everyone on the planet is against it, because you've already made up your mind without one shred of doubt. These are the types of decisions I strive for in my coaching practice, when you're so honest with yourself that your next step is 100 percent pure, right, and authentic. Man, just thinking about these amazing "aha!" moments still gives me such amazing gratification. Yes, even now, while writing this to y'all.

One Monday around 1:30 p.m., I got up from my office, walked into my director's office, asked if I could shut the door, and gave my three-week notice. I'm not sure who was happier, her or me. Regardless, there wasn't even the slightest bit of surprise or talks of reconsidering or moving to another department—it was just over. Yes, it can be that simple. I stayed professional and worked just as hard as I would have had I stayed, except I stopped working late or on weekends anymore. When people found out that I gave my notice, they kept asking me at least three times a day where I was going next, because obviously, I didn't quit a job without another one lined up, right? This is where my personality comes in, and I don't advise this for everyone, as we all have different financial situations and responsibilities. I quit without anything lined up. Given my type A, control-freak attitude, this seemed crazy, yes it did. But nothing had ever felt more right. I didn't even think about what I was going to do for those next several weeks. I just showed up to work and started to plan my travels.

Before I had given my notice, I already had a trip to Hawaii planned with some friends. I was kind of against it at first because I thought it was so cliché and romantic. Plus I wasn't going with a significant other; it was just three of my guy friends and me. Obviously, I was overruled, and so off we went to Hawaii. I knew it would be beautiful, but I wasn't expecting how spiritual and grounding it would be. Let me tell you, I love when I'm wrong about things.

We started in Maui, and then hopped over to Kona. While dining one evening, my friend Jho (Jose Antonio Hernandez—yeah, he's gonna love this plug) and I were discussing my next steps. I said I always wanted to write a book about my anxiety and start my full-time coaching business. As the conversation started to become a brainstorming session, Jho mentioned that he always wanted to write a book on Instagram and call it an Instabook. I thought about it and said that was a brilliant idea. It would have the look and feel of a book but just in a CliffsNotes version of posts. Toward the end of the conversation, he said, "I don't know when I will ever have the time or the content to write this book, so why don't you take it." And that is where my little Instabook, @afaceofanxiety, was born—in Hawaii, under the stars, among some friends having a brainstorming session. After dinner, all I could think about was this Instabook (the first of its kind), what it would look like, what my chapters would be, what it would be called. I mean, who has time to sleep when you're burning with creativity?

After Hawaii, I then went off to New Zealand to visit with my sis, Pie, and her family—more so my niece, Lells Bells. I started to write the Instabook there. I mean, my God, it's New Zealand; could I have picked a better setting? Right before I left to go back home, I did a photo shoot with an amazing photographer, Chad Wagner. Let's just say, I'm not so comfortable in front of the camera. Snapping pictures for Instagram? Sure, no problem. But a professional doing a shoot made me nervous. It's ironic that my demeanor changed when I thought about taking pictures for my book because it was for my passion project. But knowing that these pictures were going to be used to send a message, with my face representing the many faces of anxiety, made me feel more comfortable in my skin. Chad captured the exact pictures I wanted and needed for a book I hadn't even written yet, but it was so real in my heart. It's funny how people tend to come into your life exactly when you need them.

So here we are, you and I. I took a leap of faith and quit my six-figure cushy job to start my coaching practice full-time and write this book about my life with anxiety. This phase of life is where you see what you're made of, because you go broke, you invest all your money into yourself. It's a sink-or-swim environment. I've never invested in myself quite like this before, but so far, I will say that I am in true alignment with my life, my passions, and my strengths, and as my first quote states, my dysfunction has now become my function. I laugh to myself just thinking about it. Because, my whole life, I have hidden my anxiety, pushed it away, and tried to bury it over and over again, and now I just embrace the hell out of it and have made it a part of my life and career.

Key Takeaways:

- You must fail in life sometimes to succeed.
- Careers are not always carved out.
- Don't chase the money; chase the dream if you can.

Chapter 6

Relationships

"Don't wait for someone to
make you feel special
Be Special
Set the standards to receive
the love you deserve"

So here's the juicy part, right: relationships, my favorite topic. I've been in love twice in my life. Anxiety, for sure, was so present in both of these relationships. So, as previously mentioned, I refer to these men as boyfriend A and boyfriend B (BF-A and BF-B). My whole life, I had been the serial dater, mainly because it was easy to focus on someone else rather than myself. I never wanted to deal with my anxiety issues, so my boyfriends became my entire world. The problem was that at the time, I didn't even see what I was doing. Do you know how much pressure that is on the other person to carry that extreme burden of you making them your world and how dangerous it is for you to allow it to happen? Codependence was a big part of my relationships, and it happens a lot in young love. But you need to make sure you become your own person with your own identity and independence.

So my BF-A was my first big love. Sure, I dated all through high school and had multiple boyfriends. I'm pretty sure in my bequeathals (not sure they even still do that in yearbooks anymore), mine said, "A steady relationship." Yeah, as if that's not a sign, right? So I had zero interest in BF-A, but he attended the same college as I did, which was four hours away from my hometown. We were up in Massachusetts, and I would drive us both back and forth on weekends. He became one of my closest friends. We had gone to high school together, but back then, he was one of those stoners, and I was a cheerleader who hung out with what I guess back then was the "cool kids." BF-A and I were always cool with each other, and we shared a mutual love for music. I was happy to have a familiar face at college, mainly because I was in the depths of anxiety hell, trying my best to transition. BF-A was comforting, and when I was with him, I didn't feel as anxious, which is how I knew right away this was going to be bad. He wasn't anything like me; he just dealt with life as it came, while I had to plan every part of my existence. So he helped balance me out.

I soon realized I had feelings for him, and I was embarrassed to tell my friends from back home about him. We were such an extreme couple. He never had a girlfriend before me, and I was already on boyfriend number eight. We both fell hard in love and soon became inseparable. I never in a thousand-million years would have thought that I would fall in love with this guy. I mean, it's still baffling, but here we were, just two kids in love. We dated for all four years of college. I left our first school and tried out several others. He came back home with me for a moment, and then he ended up returning to our original college in Massachusetts. I drove there every weekend to see him, even with the panic attacks I would experience on the highways. He knew I had these issues, but he never made me feel bad; he just loved me. I never liked traveling, but he got me to take him to Guatemala, which I had avoided for years, but with him, I felt as though I could take on the world. So you can only imagine the devastation when, after four years, he cheated on me and left me for a girl who was just like him, did drugs, went to Phish shows—ya know, nothing like me. It felt as if someone had gutted me, like they took their bare hands and ripped my heart out. I couldn't function. I stopped eating, stopped working, and worst of all, I was recovering from an injury that left me housebound with a broken coccyx and a broken nose, all on top of a very broken heart.

My injury happened at New Year's, when I fell off a stage. No, I wasn't working the pole or anything; it was one of those freak accidents. BF-A had been at a Phish show with this girl, and that was it. He had found his next girlfriend, and I was left physically and mentally damaged. BF-A was just a guy who was living life, and I was someone who was trying to fit into his life so I could avoid living my own. I recall the times when he would go hang out with his friends and I wouldn't have any plans, so the anxiety would spike, and I thought, *this is it, this is the end.* He had to go through a lot of my anxiety swings. I did start going to a therapist while he and I were together, but I still just wasn't ready yet.

It seems so ridiculous now, as I'm such a strong, independent woman. But I think it's all of these experiences that have led me to become stronger and better equipped. There were so many times when I needed BF-A to come over to my parents' house because my attacks were so bad and I was puking and shaking, and no one else was able to soothe me. I'm not gonna lie, this took about five years to get over. Sure, I dated after him, but it wasn't until I met BF-B that I fell in love again. I went back to my usual patterns and had boyfriends, aka fillers, some of whom I even lived with. The reason I even allowed this to happen was because, again, I needed to feel needed by someone. I needed reassurance at all times. I was just so scared to be alone and deal with myself, so I would rather date anyone else to avoid it. I know I hurt many people in the process, and for that, I am truly sorry.

At this point of my life, I was already living in NYC with one of my boyfriends when I fell in love with BF-B—yep, I know, shitty, but hey, it's the truth. He wasn't even someone I thought I would like, but we worked together at the first club I spoke about. He was also nine years my senior, but somehow I had fallen for this South African man. He was married when we met, and yeah, I made some bad decisions, but it happened. BF-B and I had this uncanny connection; it was immediate. I knew together we were special, and it wasn't just me; everyone who worked with us saw it. Eventually, I left to take a different job, and thankfully, he did not come with us. We needed some separation, and I didn't want to be involved with a married man any longer. I was still living with a previous boyfriend when BF-B called to offer me an incredible opportunity in a new mega-club, but I didn't want to work with him because I just didn't trust the situation. However, he mentioned that he was separated now and it would be strictly, 100 percent professional. Well I took the nightclub job, and he was right. It was a mega-club, one that changed nightlife in its entirety, and he was running it as the GM. The first night of work, we couldn't fight the attraction. I took one look at this man and my heart knew what it wanted. It was such a chemical reaction between the two of us and, well, the short version is that I had to make the guy I was currently living with move out so that shortly after, I could move in with BF-B.

BF-B and I ran the club together as well as lived together and, to be honest, I never got sick of him. He and I had such a nice balance. I had since learned to be more independent and was spreading my wings as I found my calling as a life coach. And he was always so supportive of whatever passions I had, and I will state for the record that he always encouraged me to be a full-time coach and leave nightlife. Since he was South African, he went to visit his family for a month at a time. The first time I went with him, you would have thought he was shipping me to a desolate island where I had to fend for myself. I wasn't traveling as much back then, and one day, he just said, "Pack your bags. We're going. Get ready." This is how I found my life coach, David. I contacted him to help me get through the eighteen-hour flight to a country I knew nothing about, a place far away from my comfort zone. David said, "Well this is going to take some sessions. You're going to have to just get through it, and we'll start when you're back." Wait, what was that you said? Get through it, ugh, I just wanted a magic pill that would make my anxiety vanish! Mind you, the entire time I was with BF-B, I never experienced any anxiety or panic attacks, because our job was so mentally and physically draining that there was just no room for it. Plus I lived with him, so if something went wrong, I knew he would help me get through it or deal with it. He was a scrapper for sure, and I just felt so safe with him. I think my anxiety felt safe with him too. I want to stop here for a minute and point out that this is not how you find your person. Traveling started the panic, but since he was right there with me, I was able to just barely manage. It was a struggle for sure; I was white-knuckling it through many of those trips. But I knew if I didn't go, I would miss out on the breathtaking safaris, cheetah petting's, ostrich riding, and the endless wine tasting all through South Africa. If anything, he opened me up to wanting to travel again. He pushed me out of my comfort zone, and I managed to do it all without Xanax or any meds back then.

So here comes the devastation. We had been living together for four years and all in for about eight years. They say there's a biological clock that starts ticking at thirty. Well listen up, ladies, it's actually a real effing thing. I never thought I would be one of those women who give their boyfriend an ultimatum, but there I was. After going to the seventh wedding of the year, I turned to him one morning and said, "Just answer me, yes or no, will you ever marry me?" He simply said, "No," and I got up and made probably the most dramatic, theatrical exit ever. Being of Latin descent, I never really saw that Latina side of myself until it came out that day. For real though, even I was scared of me. There's a scene in the movie *Waiting to Exhale* where Angela Bassett finds out her husband is leaving her for his white secretary. Angela goes into his closet and starts ripping things out, just ranting about things she's so done with, but the anger and emotion and mental anguish were portrayed so well. Trust me, watch it. So this was me; this was my Angela Bassett moment, where she sets his things on fire. I didn't have that liberty, however, so I just left, never to return. I was willing to get past the never-getting-married part, but the kids were a deal breaker. My father once told me the day he met BF-B, "Fish, that man will never marry you, and he'll break your heart." So I called my dad and cried my eyes out, and asked him to get me from NYC and bring me home. With my bags in hand, I was a New York City cliché of the chick on the street, hysterically crying into a BlackBerry.

This was right before Christmas, like five days before, and I was a wreck. I wasn't eating. My family was scared to talk to me. I would sneak into bed with my sister so I wouldn't feel so alone. The anxiety was making its way through the heartache but not enough to discourage me from staying in NYC. I think I even tried to cancel Christmas, but my dad loves it too much for that to happen. I was starting to get scared of being alone, and I would tag along with Pie everywhere. She would even drop me off at her friends' houses because she was scared to leave me alone too. I mean, WTF, right? This was crazy! It was far worse than the BF-A experience. I never thought I could laugh again or feel happiness again, and what sucked even more was that we worked together. So I still needed to make money and work alongside him, which was horrific. We didn't know how to break up; we just knew how to drive each other mad at that point. Even though I wasn't as codependent on BF-B as I was with BF-A, this was a different type of pain. I was older now, and I sincerely thought he was my soul mate, my ride or die. I didn't have a plan B because I was sure as hell we were always going to be together. Had he asked me to move into a cardboard box, I would have. I was willing to go to the end of the world for this man. I thought he was the one.

I moved in with my bestie for a month and then moved into a crappy, roach-infested apartment on the cusp of Chinatown, mainly because it was close to my old apartment with BF-B and I so wasn't ready to let go yet. The thing about anxiety is that it keeps you super attached to certain things so that you cannot look beyond them. I was living in this amazing, beautiful box with my soul mate, and that was all I knew. It had four walls and was comfortable, and I didn't need to look outside that box because there was nothing out there for me. Having BF-B break my heart was one of the most enlightening teaching periods of my life. It showed me my insecurities, my boundaries, my limits, and most of all, my fears. The breakup was neither simple nor cut-and-dry by any means. I mean, two people who cared deeply for one another but wanted to drive each other crazy wasn't healthy or mature in any way. I knew finding another job was necessary, and I did at another club away from my friends, living in a crap apartment, learning how to live alone—alone with myself, my thoughts, and my fat cat, Mia.

In my lifetime, I can honestly say these were the two biggest loves of my life. I never thought in a million years I would be writing about them, and neither did they. No worries, however, they gave me their consent for writing them into my book. I'm friendly with both of them now. There is no residual longing or hoping to be with either one. I'm not the same girl I was back when I dated them. Today I am a woman, one who is independent and sure of her needs and desires. I do run into them from time to time. One is overseas, and the other is nowhere near the city, so I never actually see much of them, but we're always friendly and cordial when we do meet. They both will forever hold a special place in my heart, but my heart no longer holds onto them. Does that make sense? We have all changed. That's the nature of evolution, and that's the beauty of love; it can come and go, but you never stop trying to find it.

I do want to discuss what kept me in these relationships longer than necessary, and that's HOPE. I do feel that hope is great, and as human beings, we should always have hope—hope for our world and ourselves. But when it comes to hoping for other people, that's where I have to wave a red flag. The moment one "HOPES" their partner will come around, be different, or give them what they finally deserve, that's when things get convoluted. No one can change unless they want to. No matter how much you "HOPE" they will change their mind or their actions, all you're doing is prolonging the inevitable. One must first learn to accept the facts of the relationship, which is why it ended in the first place. Listen to the words of your partner because all you need to know are the words coming out of their mouth. It sounds simple, right, like why wouldn't I listen to what they're saying? But trust me, when you fall in love, you will be everything but logical. I always say, stick to the facts and never assume what someone else may think or feel. You are not in the head of your partner. All you will be doing is making up stories that may or may not be true, and it only causes more unneeded distress. So do yourself a favor and listen to what people say; hear them out. If it becomes too emotional, step away so you can be clearheaded. The heart is a powerful muscle; it can overpower you at times.

Relationships aren't easy, and they never will be. It's based on relating to one another; that's where the whole word is derived from. People can't always be on the same wavelength: we grow; we aspire; we change; and we're in constant ebb and flow. Sometimes our partners grow with us or sometimes farther apart from us. If there is one guarantee I can give, it's that there are no guarantees in life. Sorry, but that's the truth, my friend. You have to just keep listening to your truth and your gut to guide you. If you can't hear your truth, then stay still and calm until you do. Speaking from emotion or anxiety is not your truth, even though you may be able to convince yourself at the moment that it is. Sometimes we need to get a reaction or feel like we've been heard, even when all that does is cause more drama and strain to the relationship. I find that writing how I feel gives me the outlet I need, and sometimes that outlet is ballet or riding my motorcycle. I don't care what it is as long as I can find inner peace. I'm still working on the whole meditation thing. It's hard for me, but I still keep trying. Find what makes you happy, what keeps you grounded, and that is one of the best practices you can give yourself, almost as a gift.

Key Takeaways:

- Stick to the facts.
- Never assume.
- Get grounded.

Chapter 7

Triggers

"There are many paths to choose
Lesson to be learned
Challenges to face
And tears that have fallen
Through it all I've chosen to
stand in my truth
For the truth is all I know"

This may be hard for some of you because sometimes reading about someone else's triggers may spike yours. So if you need to come back to this chapter, then do so. It's going to be right here in case you want to see if we have any in common or if it's relatable. Anxiety isn't a one-size-fits-all. I use this term a lot because it's so valid. Anxiety is almost like snowflakes; each one is so specific and designed differently.

My triggers are when my stomach begins to feel off; this means whenever I eat too fast, wait too long to eat, have an upset stomach, or have too much dairy. My digestive system needs to be on point at all times for me to feel okay. I have had two horrible cases of food poisoning, one that put me in the hospital and I thought I was either going to give birth to an alien or die there. Because anxiety can spike so quickly, it launches some people into catastrophic thinking. Like every time I feel something isn't quite right in my stomach, my next thought is, *OMG, I have food poisoning. This is it can I survive another one? Who's around to take me to the hospital?* I start those obsessive "what if" thoughts and go down the spiral of despair with every stomach scenario I can think of. What's funny is that even writing this makes my stomach tense up.

Even what I put into my body is an issue. I have to be very careful about what I'm eating. I never have fried foods, even French fries. Maybe I could eat several, but no more, because I know I'll be running to the bathroom since it hits me quite fast. Many people have said, "Oh, that can't be it. It can't hit your digestive system that quickly." Oh really, wanna bet? I have spent years figuring out what works for my system and what my body is even able to process, but more on that in "Treatments" chapter. The pain in my stomach sends a direct signal to my brain that something is wrong, and the sirens just go off then. I can now convince myself to be calm enough to understand that this is not hospital-warranted and just take some deep breaths and some supplements to ease the digestive process.

I need to be so very careful when drinking. I do take anti-anxiety meds every night. They're only 5 mg, but it can still make the effects of alcohol very powerful. I learned this the hard way when I was on 10 mg of Lexapro and I drank. I would start to lose my memory and have no recollection of things that had been said. I knew where I was and who I was with, but the conversations were foggy. This was a trigger too, because not remembering made me scared. Also, the next day after drinking, I would experience huge bouts of anxiety, coming in waves. Alcohol is a depressant, which has a huge impact on your mood and chemical makeup. When I say drinking, it was barely just more than three drinks that would put me over the edge, so we aren't even talking about multiple drinks here. Now, since my dosage has been lowered and I'm slowly getting off them, having three drinks is okay with my memory. However, it still affects my anxiety, so I know I'll be sensitive and I need to check in with my anxiety and know it can start at any minute. I do love my wine and wine bars with my bestie, so I make sure I always eat before or while drinking. Everything in moderation is okay, but ideally, drinking is really bad for anxiety sufferers. I would be lying if I said I'll stop drinking socially. I just make sure I'm prepared for higher levels of anxiety, and I keep hydrated. It's your body, and you should know it best.

Some anxiety suffers are very sensitive to things they see or hear. Scary movies are a huge no for me. Even trailers of movies can spike my anxiety. It scares the hell out of me, and I will climb the walls to get out of there and need to sleep next to someone for weeks to get over it. What's interesting is that I think what is happening in the movie will start happening to me too. Pie was always into scary movies. My parents didn't understand the ratings and what they meant, so Pie would make me watch *The Shining*, *Children of the Corn*, *The Exorcist*, *The Birds*, and *The Amityville Horror*—it was just awful. I may still have trauma due to those films. Once, I tried to stay with my friend's family in the Hamptons when I was in middle school, and the house was next to a cornfield. So when we all tried to go to bed, I started to have a panic attack and called my parents. My dad and Pie were in the car for a three-hour ride to come collect me. As you can see, scary movies are definitely not my thing. Thanks a lot, Pie. As an adult, I don't even test myself. I do like a show called *Hoarders*, but I can only watch one episode; any more than that and the anxiety spikes. My anxiety has made me a clean freak, but I'm not a diagnosed OCD, more so OCD tendencies. I find the show *Hoarders* fascinating, and it's great to watch on a weekend because it gives me so much motivation to clean my apartment from top to bottom.

Hospitals give me severe panic since people who are ill, have diseases, or were in accidents surround me. Rationally, I understand that the chances of catching anything are very slim to none. I can say this to myself all I want, but the moment I walk into a hospital, my anxiety starts that vicious cycle of catastrophic thinking. Once, BF-B had almost power washed his hand off, and I was called to come collect him from the hospital. I walked in there so concerned and wanted to make sure he was okay, but as soon as I saw him lying there and saw the other people in the waiting rooms and all the sick people around me, I started to get nauseous and had a full-blown panic attack. I started to throw up in the sink in the room. The nurses had to take BF-B off the hospital bed to lay me down. They were asking me all sorts of questions, and I was just so anxious that I said I had to leave. BF-B was so angry that I had come, and instead of helping out, I had just caused more drama and had to be escorted out. So I left him there and went home to bed. So, as you can see, I am not the person you call when you're in the hospital. However, on the flip side, if you are in a crisis, then yes, you want me there. I am so efficient and rational. I can go with anyone to the hospital if I'm at the scene where the crisis happened, because I've already gone into survivor mode and now I am solely focused on their well-being. Clearly, it doesn't make any sense. It's all mind over matter, and over the years, I have gotten better.

An interesting one is that extremely intoxicated people give me anxiety. Now, working in nightlife and running clubs for all those years, you would think I'd be used to it by now. But no, it can still get to me. And not like drunk fun people, more like the people where you think to yourself, *OMG, how is that person still functioning or walking or talking?* The reason it spikes my anxiety is because I think of the crazy anxiety I would have if I were ever that drunk. Now, I'm also not saying I've been a saint either. C'mon, I ran nightclubs. So yes, there have been times when I was overserved, and trust me, those hangovers with insane amounts of panic were enough to scare me away from drinking for a while. A few times, I even had to call someone over because the anxiety was sending me into crazy spirals and I was afraid to be alone. These days, I'm more kind to my body and acknowledge how horrible the next day could be. So I need to remind myself to have only three glasses of wine or no more than two cocktails of hard liquor. Aging has also affected my intake of alcohol, so the combination of old age and anxiety puts a damper on my drinking. But on a more positive note, I feel better, and I'm far more productive than I've ever been. Again, just to remind you guys, I am nowhere near an alcoholic. All I want to do is just let you know about the severity of drinking with anxiety.

The last trigger is probably the biggest, because I encounter it so often, and that's traveling. I could be traveling without even getting on a plane. Just going away for the weekend to somewhere I haven't been can spike the anxiety. I'm always super excited when I'm packing and getting ready. But then, when I get to my destination, usually around dinnertime, I start to feel the waves of panic. I'm not so sure why it's centered on food. But usually, I'll be really hungry, and then when I sit down and start eating, I'll begin to feel these waves of uncertainty come over me, and then comes the catastrophic thinking. *Oh God, what's happening with my stomach? What if I have a panic attack? Will I get food poisoning from eating this?* If there are more than three people at the table, the waves come on even stronger. It's like my hearing is acuter and I can hear people chewing and drinking—it just starts to drive me nuts. This only becomes an issue when I'm traveling, because I'm so sensitive to new places. In my head, I feel as though I'm out of my comfort zone, and therefore, perhaps I'm unsafe.

Aside from the eating part, my body and mind are so hyperaware/hypersensitive that if I'm not close to my apartment, or something I know that's familiar, I am then automatically in unsafe zones where anxiety is lurking around every corner. Trust me, guys, I know this is untrue, but my brain has been hardwired to think and feel this way. I'll go into more detail about what I do now to counteract these thoughts in the "Treatments" chapter. Even going to Guatemala, where I travel every three months, can trigger waves of anxiety and panic attacks. There isn't a rhyme or reason why this happens. Sometimes I'm fine and feel zero anxiety at all when I'm there, and other times it can be back-to-back panic attacks every day. When I was younger, having to go to Guatemala may have given me PTSD for sure. And I'm not just throwing that term around loosely; I'm serious. Being made to go to Guatemala for months at a time was just so brutal on my nervous system that I conditioned myself to feel this way every time I had to travel somewhere else. Now, this isn't to say that I don't get panic or anxiety at my apartment. I do, but those are always triggered by a stomach symptom.

I laugh at myself because it's ironic that I hate to travel and yet I do it so often. Some people even ask if I've moved to Guatemala and come back to New York to visit. Never did I expect to have to go back and forth so often, but you know what? Life doesn't go as planned. I never married BF-B. I live in New York City. And I ran an eighty-seven-acre farm with my dad and bought two horses this year. So you see what I mean; everything's just so crazy. Sometimes I'm totally chill on the flight to wherever I'm going, and other times I need to take half a Xanax to handle the turbulence, which no matter what will always send me into a cosmic panic because I have the worst g-force. (Is that how you even say that?) Basically, I can never go on amusement park rides because the g-force of the up and down from the roller coasters is a danger to me. I will seriously try to jump out of whatever type of machine I've crawled into. I used to go on rides when I was younger because I succumbed to peer pressure. But now, when people are like, "OMG, it's so fun, let's go to XYZ park," I just say, "Nope, not me." I'll be anywhere else but there, thank you very much!

Also, confined spaces can trigger me—pretty sure most people have this. But this just adds to why flying gets me so revved up, because if I think too deeply about the fact that I'm enclosed in a tin object, suspended in air, and I can't get off even when I want to, that just makes my thoughts spiral out of control. I've had most of these concerns my whole life. The only new thing that popped up was the food poisoning, because I didn't know you could experience death without actually dying. I'll continue dealing with all of these triggers of mine because that is all they are: just triggers. *Trigger*, by definition, is *the cause of a situation or event*. All these triggers have been something I've learned to be scared of, and I've trained my body to fear these situations, no matter how many times I've survived them.

<u>Key Takeaways:</u>

- Triggers are learned.
- Life has no guarantees.
- Get to know your triggers as well as possible.

Chapter 8

Treatments

"It's ok to ask for help:
From the Universe
From your Mentors
From your Tribe
Ask and it is given"

Yes! Finally, what you guys have been waiting for this entire book, or maybe you skipped ahead. Regardless, yay, we're here! So I want to preface again that not all anxiety or panic disorder is the same. Some methods have worked for me but may not help your specific triggers, which is why I wanted to discuss what my mine were first. We also process information differently. Some people are visual, auditory, auditory digital, or kinesthetic. Are you asking yourself what the hell the difference is between all these? No worries, I got you. Here are the definitions in layman's terms.

Visual is when people memorize and learn by seeing pictures and tend to be less distracted by noise than others. They tend to have difficulty remembering and are bored during long, verbal presentations, because their minds will wander. Auditory processors are easily distracted by noise and learn by listening. Vocal tone and quality are important to them, to get them to focus. Auditory-digital people spend a good amount of time in their heads, talking to themselves. They memorize and learn by steps, procedures, and sequences. Kinesthetic people often speak very low; they are more oriented toward their feelings as compared to all the people in the other categories mentioned. They learn by actively doing something and by learning the actual feeling for it. They are interested in what "feels right" or gives them a "gut feeling." Have you figured out which one you are yet? It's good to know this about yourself because, maybe, if this had been on audio, it would have been easier for you to process. Or perhaps my picture on the cover is what drew you into purchasing this book. Whatever the reason and whatever process work for you, it's good to know which one of these four elements you are. I'm kinesthetic—aside from the fact that I don't speak quietly, but I used to when I was younger. I was quite the shy one.

Okay, so we know how to process; now let's get to what worked for me. So when I finally quit nightlife and accepted the offer with the big liquor company, I knew I was screwed because I never managed my anxiety well, which is why I hired a therapist. I saw her for about a year. We never discussed medication because I was highly against it, and since I was already in my early thirties, I figured that if I got this far, why bother now. I always tell people to find a therapist that vibes with them, because you need to make sure you know what type of therapist they are, what their background is, and whether they are specialized in what you need them for. The first therapist I saw was just to keep me in my job. But once I moved passed that, I was still left with a lot of underlying anxiety, so I went out and found someone better suited for me. I can't tell you enough how many people make the mistake of seeing one therapist and not trying out others. There are way too many different types of therapists, too long even to write down, but please do your research. Back to my therapist, I found him through a work colleague, not a close enough colleague that it was an issue but close enough for me to take his referral seriously. So I started seeing my therapist, who specialized in anxiety by way of CBT (cognitive behavioral therapy and talk therapy). When I first started seeing him, he mentioned getting on anti-anxiety meds, which I politely declined. I did have a Xanax script from my regular physician due to my frequent panic attacks, so I was comfortable just knowing I had those.

I started therapy, and one Sunday evening, I went to see *Silver Linings Playbook* with a friend. I can honestly say that if there was one movie that changed my entire life, that was it. Thanks, David O. Russell (the director). So I saw the film, and afterward, my friend asked if I knew anyone with a mental disorder. I just sat down and immediately started to cry. He didn't know what the hell was happening, and I told him, through tears of shame, that I was the one with a disorder. The next morning, I spoke to one of my besties and asked her about meds and whether she ever took anything to help her. She was so supportive and told me to take something so I could clear my head and get to the root of the problem. So, Tuesday afternoon, I walked into my therapist's office and asked for medication. I now had to be seen by a psychiatrist who, luckily, was next door, as they worked closely together. This was when I started taking Lexapro 5 mg. I was so embarrassed about taking meds that I didn't tell anyone except those close to me. The first two weeks sucked—I felt so off and almost gave up—because your body has to acclimate to the medication, and that part is super tough. Still, I hung in there and finally started to feel lighter and less anxious. It wasn't a high dose, but I'm on the small side and my body is very sensitive to any form of medication, so it worked like magic. I'm still on the same dose, and this coming fall, I'll be tapering off and just keeping Xanax for emergencies. Just an FYI, your alcohol tolerance will change when you're on this, or at least it did for me—two or three drinks and I was already drunk. At first, I couldn't remember most conversations I had when I was drinking, and that scared the hell out of me. So I started drinking less frequently and made sure I never pushed it, so that's kind of a bonus, because now I'm such a lightweight.

I also check in with my life coach now and then. He got me to see things more clearly and face situations that I pretended weren't there. He was the reason I found my calling because I loved how he coached and the vocabulary he used. He has been coaching for over thirty-two years; he's a goddamn pioneer of coaching. Thanks, David Dowd, for everything. I was finally able to leave the things that were no longer serving me, and I also took notice of my use of negative language that was holding me back. I have been seeing David for ten-plus years; he has been on my journey with me. He helped when I first started taking coaching classes at NYU. He guided me in my decision to leave a relationship that was never going to serve me, as well as freezing my eggs so that I had a backup plan in case life got in the way and my window closed. Now I always have the option of my backup, younger eggs. Ain't modern science great? Ladies, FREEZE YOUR EGGS!!!!

Another form of treatment I love and have been doing since 2000 is acupuncture; this is such a great anxiety relief. But again, please make sure you do your research because there is a significant difference in forms and treatments. Luckily, I have a sister who is a gifted acupuncturist; however, the downside is that she lives in NZ. But while she was here Stateside, I was able to learn the difference between good treatments and great ones. I find acupuncture to be very spiritual, and I need to vibe with my person and have some deep connection. I've been seeing Robert Paul Johnson for some time now, and he is one of the gifted ones. There are so many points to access for anxiety, and plus he also recommends herbs too. I pick them up in Chinatown at Kamwo, which if you didn't know about before, now you do, so you're welcome. I follow a very strict protocol of herbs for my cycle, as it throws my hormones off, and yep, you guessed it, it throws off my anxiety. I could probably write an entire chapter on why acupuncture works for me, but I'll try to keep it short and simple.

Acupuncture makes me feel grounded and less flighty. My sis will even put seeds in my ear when I head back on the plane to the States so I don't panic. Again, I don't have any terminology because I'm not a student of Chinese medicine, but as a patient, this was one of the most eye-opening revelations. Originally, I went to a practicing acupuncture school in Syosset, Long Island, to see if it would help me with my digestive issues and weight loss. After a few sessions of being poked and prodded by the students of the school, I soon realized that this really made me a lot calmer and levelheaded. I ended up bringing Pie with me to a session, and just like that, she found her calling and became an amazing acupuncturist living in NZ. So, as you see, acupuncture has been in my life for many years of trial and error, and finding the right people, not only from a medical standpoint but also from a spiritual one.

My next favorite healer is my homeopathic doctor, who I only found during the past three years due to my ulcers and IBS issues. She shed some light on how my stomach was able to break food down and what exactly was being absorbed into my body and what wasn't. She had me take a series of tests, and when all was done, I had a list of supplements that helped with my anxiety and also treated my gut so that it wouldn't trigger any panic attacks. Here's a list of what I take daily:

- Probiotics
- Vitamin D, B12, B6
- L-5-MTHF
- L-Theanine

Here is what she provided me with for when I travel, so I can feel prepared if I encounter any food I can't eat or if it's something worse, like an upset stomach or food poisoning:

- Oil of Oregano pills
- Charcoal pills
- Beef Protein powder for shakes
- Probiotics

Now let me remind y'all that this is very specific to my body and what I can and cannot absorb, so it won't be the same for everyone who has anxiety. I'm not going to sit here and lie to you either and say that seeing a homeopathic is cheap; it sure as hell is not. Pretty sure, all in all, my total for tests and consulting with supplements was somewhere around $3K or $4K. And yes, you can write them off, as this isn't covered under insurance. However, who knows what our health system is going to look like in the future, so I'm mentioning it just to mention it. I like to be as transparent as possible because these are the questions I get most often, and I never like surprises when I'm trying to find the right treatment plan. Since I started seeing my homeopath, I haven't had any ulcers come back, and when I taper off the Lexapro, this is the only way I'll go.

Another question I get a lot is whether or not taking supplements is good for you. Okay, so look, I know my body is unable to process certain foods, so why not give it the nutrients that it's lacking? Plus there are so many correlations between gut health and anxiety. I want to make sure I'm keeping a healthy and happy gut environment to keep the anxiety at bay.

Last but not least is exercise. This is probably the most valuable thing to do to keep anxiety in check. I started going back to ballet, as I have been dancing since I was three years old. I stopped after BF-B because, well, I was just so in it and miserable. But the moment I put those tights and the leotard back on and started going to Joffrey Ballet School, my whole mindset changed.

Here is what I can say about exercise: Find something that you love, something that moves your body but in a way that your mind can shift. I have a very overactive brain, so I need something that will have me concentrating on my breath and my core, so that I am fully engaged and present. Ballet encompasses all of this. You have to keep beats and steps in your head, not forget to breathe, and watch your form. So by the time I leave class, I can't even recall what I was anxious about. Dance, to me, is what I need to de-stress. I'm just in the moment with the piano and concentrating on my posture, and it all just turns out to be so therapeutic. Now, do I expect everyone to go out and start dancing ballet? No I don't. You have to find what works for you. I always tell people that ballet and riding my Ducati Monster 900 (motorcycle) put me in the same mindset. So, you see, it can be something different than dance. When I'm riding my bike, Hunter, I have to be aware of my posture and my breath. I have to look at the turns ahead of me; my mind can't be anywhere else but in the present. The moment I'm distracted or unsure is when mistakes happen. Wherever you're looking is where you're going. If you look ahead of you, that's where you will stay. Trust me, I know from experience that if you look down, down you will go, my friend.

Think about all the things that keep you in the present—not in the past or the future, but the present, in this exact moment—because that's where we anxiety sufferers don't live very often. I'll admit that I'm not great at meditating, so I often have to do classes that can help me along. I'm obsessed with Y7 Studio yoga in NYC; it's a hip-hop yoga class that's taught in a candlelit hot room—not to be confused with Bikram Yoga, which is hot as hell and I would probably die. Y7 yoga is hot enough for me to sweat out all my toxins, sweat out the anxiety, and force me to breathe deep and stretch. I found it by accident when I had food poisoning and both my besties told me to take a yoga class to help shift my thinking. Lo and behold, it was a hot-yoga class, which makes it even better because I like the sweaty part; it's great for your body and mind.

In addition I frequently take barre3 class because it combines ballet and resistance. It's literally the perfect combination of my skills and hobbies. It get's me toned while making my body stronger, with instructors I adore so win win for me. Before I discovered all these classes I used to belong to a conglomerate gym that was super expensive. But I realized, like most Americans, that I disliked going to the gym and never got motivated enough to really commit to it. Now that I only take classes, I go with my girlfriends and I really love attending all of them and find connecting to the instructors a key part of committing to a regime. Sometimes just deciding which one to go to is the biggest hurdle. So listen, you don't have to pound it out at the gym or do a marathon. Just find your thing, and once you find it, you'll want to do it often, and that's all that matters.

Recently I have been taking meditation at The Path in NYC, where they guide you gently into breathing and sitting with stillness at a group session. It's a small group of like-minded people, so I resonate with it. It taught me that the best thing for people with anxiety, especially when you're in the middle of a panic attack, is to re-center and focus on your inhale and exhale. So what has worked for me so far is saying the words while I do the action. When I inhale, I say in my head, "I am inhaling." Then on the exhale, I say, "I am exhaling." The reason why saying it to yourself helps is because it blocks all the unnecessary, negative talk that starts happening when you get anxious and begin to panic. You have to shift your mindset and not spiral to the catastrophic thinking that anxiety loves to do. Easier said than done, which is why it's important to practice before you're thrown into that situation.

What's hard for anxiety sufferers such as myself is that we often feel unsafe and scared. I'm learning that it's not my apartment that makes me safe, nor is it Chelsea, Manhattan, that gives me security or safety. I am safe wherever I am because I am the vessel that houses my spirit and soul. The fact that we make certain locations "safe" is just untrue, but we have trained our brains to think that way. I know this may sound so simple to some of you and super complicated to others. I always lived my life scared of the world, scared of what was to come and all that could happen. And let me tell you, that is just no way to live, man. I white-knuckled it through most of my entire life, until my therapist said, "Does it have to be this hard? Are you winning something at the end for enduring so much pain and turmoil over something you could just take a pill for and learn how to cope with better?" Well goddamn it, yeah, he was right. Why was I white-knuckling it through life and for whom? No one even knew what I was going through, so I just suffered in silence. Well no more of that silence. Because now all that pain and struggle have become this book you're reading, which can hopefully give some of you the peace you are seeking or the courage to do something about it.

Key Takeaways:

- It's okay to ask for help.
- Medication can be a useful tool to get grounded.
- Be kind to your body, and give it the attention and love it

Chapter 9

Finding Balance

"Learn from your mistakes
And own them
Open your heart
And respect others
Build a business
And mind your own"

Oh, I love this chapter because this is probably the hardest thing I ever had to find in my life. What is a balance, and how do you get it? Well if it was only that simple! Start off with what's easy and review your life right now: What feels off about it to you? And it doesn't have to be anxiety related either, because all my issues in life sure as hell weren't. I needed to find a balance between my life, work, relationships, and even my parents. I had to take a hard look at my life and ask myself the hard questions: "Trish, what do you want?" Then after you ask yourself this, you also have to actually figure it out. Sometimes what we thought we always wanted isn't what really makes us most happy or fulfilled.

I left the security of money to go out on my own and take a risk. Even writing this book is a risk because, to be honest, I didn't think so many people would read it on Instagram. I chose to share something so personal that I didn't share with anyone for many years, and here I am putting it all out there for people to read. So, you see, we never know how things will end up; they just end up happening if only you allow things to unfold.

All my life, I've been a control freak. I wanted to know when, why, and how much. Anxiety created a pattern to control all aspects of my life so I could figure out how to deal with them and avoid any surprises. Just writing this makes me laugh because I don't know whom I was kidding. I drove some people nuts, that's for damn sure. The only person I was hurting the most this entire time was myself. It's a funny concept that we always tend to hurt ourselves the most. It has taken many therapy sessions, self-help books, psychology classes, and lots and lots of dance to get to the point I'm at right now. Right now, all I know is that I have my coaching practice and I'm writing a book. Beyond that, I don't have anything figured out, and that's okay. It doesn't plague me anymore. I researched the things to eat that are right for my body and my anxiety. There is a plethora of knowledge out there for you to read or join, which can make this a much easier experience. I mean, just having a social media platform where people talk about mental health is huge. If you're struggling to ask for help, if you're confused to ask the right questions, if you're scared, then go deep and become the person you need for yourself.

For most of my adolescent years, I looked toward my boyfriends to balance me out, to make me feel safe and wanted. The Universe was hell bent that I figure out this lesson the hard way. So take some advice from someone who's been in the depths of hell with anxiety, and go inward. You be the person who gets you through the hard times, through the anxiety and panic, because you're always with yourself and you're the one who also creates your mental prison. Get to know your anxiety the way you would a new lover; ask questions to get connected, to become closer to its ways. This may seem stupid now, but trust me, sometimes it's easier to push it away and run from it because we're too scared to face it. I should know—I did it for almost thirty-four years, until I had enough.

Even though anxiety can make day-to-day life difficult, there are other things about it that help make me who I am. What's funny is that I was worried to start taking the anti-anxiety meds for fear it would change who I was, because I like who I am. But happily, it didn't; it just takes a little off the edge. I am always a prompt person, very detail oriented, and pretty much a perfectionist to some degree, with tendencies of OCD—not full blown but just tiny tendencies. All of these descriptions are things that I love about myself; I never want them to change. Being organized and on top of things has made me excel in my career endeavors and continues to make me strive for success. So yes, anxiety sucks, but it's also not all that bad either once you take the fear away. We are complex people with complex anatomies. So do your research. Find out how your body works and what you can do to make sure you're living life to the absolute fullest.

I can't remember the exact year, but for Christmas one year, I started a tradition to write down what we wanted to bring in for the New Year and place it on pretty nametags, the same ones you would use for a present. Once everyone had written theirs down, we hung them on the Christmas tree. And after the season had passed, we then hung everyone's up in someone's home. Ours goes on my vision board. The following year, we place them on the tree, along with the new ones, and we can see through the years what we've manifested and if it came true. Three years ago, mine said "balance," and after about 1.5 years, I finally have it. I know life is always changing, and that's okay. I love that about life. But now that I feel more secure with my thoughts, and myself, I feel balanced enough to deal with it, no matter what pops up. My friends and family have noticed a big difference in me. I'm not carrying around the weight of the world on my shoulders, and you shouldn't either. Ask yourself, who put it there? Yeah, you did, at some point when you weren't looking. So take it off. Leave that to some higher power, and just focus on what you can change, and that should be your mindset.

Everything feeds into everything. So watch what you put into your system, what you're reading, who you spend your time with, etc. You may think these things don't matter, but they do. I asked myself a few years back, "If I was on my deathbed, would I be thinking about my anxiety, or would I be wondering why I didn't do the things I always wanted to do but was always too scared to do? What will my legacy be?" I'm on the older side regarding having babies, but let's say I don't have children. Is there anything I'm leaving behind? After all these years, I can finally say yes. This little book, which started as a brainstorming session on a beach in Hawaii, will be what I leave behind, my words and my life voyage through this crazy world with anxiety/panic disorder. This book has brought me balance and courage to be the person I was hiding from for a very long time. I am living my true authentic life. Even though my past has been super colorful, I wouldn't change my current life for anything in the world. Over the course of our lives, we bend and grow into something else. This is my something else. Take a crappy situation and make lemonade. That's right, look at Beyoncé; she made a whole goddamn album about it. So find your balance. Find what's right for you and your life, not what's right for anyone else. Because we're born alone, and we'll die alone; that's the nature of the world. So get to know yourself best before anyone else, and love the hell out of yourself.

Key Takeaways:

- Balance: that's the key to life, your path to happiness.
- You are safe.
- Be your support system.

Chapter 10

Acceptance and Moving Forward

"When you're brave enough
to take your blinders off
that's when the world
opens up to you"

Here we are, at the end of our journey together. Man, are you guys just as exhausted as I am? The question I get over and over again is, "How do you overcome this disorder?" If anyone had that answer or secret, trust me, none of us would even be in the position we are right now, possibly not even reading this book, because there wouldn't have been any need to write it. There isn't a "quick fix," a precious pill, or a miracle retreat. Sorry, but it's true. You need first to accept that this is part of your life, part of what you are, so just focus on moving forward regardless.

My biggest challenge was that I just didn't want to accept the disorder. I wanted to bury it away somewhere deep inside and deal with it only when needed. Now that I dove headfirst into understanding my specific triggers and found the right medication for myself, it's just a matter of managing it. I often find that we spend too much time in our heads, trying to analyze every step of the way, just over thinking it all. When you place all your attention onto just one thing, well then that one thing will get amplified and consume every part of you. Your anxiety loves when you do this. Do you want to give your anxiety that satisfaction? I allow anxiety to be with me because I'm not scared of it popping up anymore. It takes less energy just to notice what's beside you than worrying the whole time when it will show up. Sometimes anxiety doesn't show up at all because I'm just not putting all my thoughts and control toward it.

We all hear of self-fulfilling prophecies; this would be doing exactly that. The moment you say to yourself, "I hope I don't get a panic attack. I hope I don't have anxiety the whole time," that's a clear invitation. You just asked it to join you, front row, VIP seats and all. The more energy you give to something the more power it has, right? So, as Rage Against the Machine would say, "We gotta take the power back," and that has been my mantra for the past several years. Anxiety may have dictated my life as a youngster, but now, hell no! This is my life, and I dictate how I live it and why I live it. If you had asked me even five years ago whether I would be traveling back and forth to Guatemala this often, working for myself, and running a farm, I would have thought you were crazy—'cause it's such a far-fetched idea. Now I don't even flinch if someone tells me I have to pack my bags and we're going to Nepal, meh, okay, let's do it.

So, you see, I don't check in with my anxiety first to see what it tells me to do. Now I just tell it what I'm doing instead, and either it'll come along or it won't. I still deal with anxiety and panic attacks whenever they pop up, and I find the best way to deal with them at that moment. Then I start my next day as if nothing ever happened. This is very important, and I cannot stress it enough. You can't just get caught up in bad moments. So you had anxiety and possibly a bad panic attack. You need to let it go and not let these moments ruin the next day, week, or possibly even months. Let's throw it back to Newton's Law (yes, physics): "An object in motion tends to stay in motion." So if you keep giving anxiety more movement, more power, then it's going to stay in motion, stay in your head and body. Do whatever it is you can do to push your way out of that space. This is where you refer to the "Treatments" chapter and find some ways to shift your thinking.

I'm really big on analogies, so here's one of my favorite ones to use. And mind you, this is for those who don't suffer from alcoholism. When you first started drinking, I'm sure there was a point where you got drunk and very sick, and you promised God or some holy spirit that never again would you drink if they could just save you from this agony right now. The next day, you're just happy you survived, and a few days later, you feel great, and you're like, "Yeah, let's grab some drinks." Why is it so easy to get past that drunken sickness where you prayed and vowed never to do it again, but yet here you are, excited to have some social cocktails with friends? I'll tell you why: You now know you can survive. You know the cause of the agony that is to follow, and the effects of it too. It's a learned response that the alcohol will leave your system and, at some point, you will go back to feeling better. You need to apply this same way of thinking to your anxiety. You will survive. You may experience it again, but you can't stop living your life. So enjoy the moments, and just be present. There will be good days and bad days, for sure. Just don't beat yourself up when it gets tough.

Another sensitive issue is when you speak to people who just don't seem to understand you or your anxiety. I have found that it's best not to force it on others; don't try to make anyone understand it fully. Those who are interested will find out, one way or another, what the illness is. To those who are close to us, like family, friends, and partners, I will just say this: It's like politics, and everyone has their view so we'll just agree to disagree. Mental illness doesn't look the same for everyone, and most people misuse the statements "I'm having anxiety" or "I had a panic attack" when they can't find anything to wear or their loved one didn't text back within five milliseconds. This causes so much confusion and demeans the illness for those of us who do suffer from the disorder. Always take things with a grain of salt, fight for things worth fighting for, and don't allow the ignorance of others to bring you down.

Before writing my Instabook, which has now become this actual book, I never spoke a word about my anxiety except with maybe four people in my life. Now I have strangers talking to me about their struggles, which is exactly what I wanted, except I didn't know that until now. I started out this book with a quote that states, "My dysfunction has now become my function," and truer words have never been spoken. I have made my career based around what I have been scared of my whole life. I don't think everyone will go out and start writing a book, but the point is that when we embrace the parts of us that scare us the most, sometimes greatness will come out of it. I do feel my anxiety lessen with every word I write, but that's my journey, and it's been my way of healing. I love speaking about my work and this book because it makes me proud to read how far I have come.

To continue reading about my journey follow me on IG @afaceofanxiety where this passion project the #instabook started.

I leave you with these final questions -

What's your story?

How does your story change your future?

What will you leave behind?

Never the end, always a new beginning

Trish Barillas has been a Life Coach for over a decade, coaching on Anxiety, Relationships, Breakups and Job Advancements. Author of the first ever Instabook, @afaceofanxiety, that started on Instagram.

Trish has been living with anxiety/panic disorder since the age of 5 years old. The Guatemalan-American has a strong passion for helping others. Barillas is the founder of 3GS Charity (Gifts and Goals for Guatemala) where she helps raise funds for rural villages in Guatemala, as well as her participation in mentorships with New York City high school students. Barillas also manages a cattle and lime farm with her father in Guatemala.

Trish likes to call herself a "creator of positive change and a goal pusher" in her own words.

NOTES:

NOTES:

Made in the USA
Las Vegas, NV
23 August 2023